Assault from the Sea

The Amphibious Landing at Inchon

by Curtis A. Utz

No. 2

The U.S. Navy in the Modern World Series

Series Editor
Edward J. Marolda
Head, Contemporary History Branch

Naval Historical Center
Department of the Navy
Washington
1994

Secretary of the Navy's
Advisory Committee on Naval History

Library of Congress Cataloging-in-Publication Data

Utz, Curtis A., 1962–
    Assault from the sea : the amphibious landing at Inchon / by
Curtis A. Utz.
      p.   cm. — (The U.S. Navy in the modern world series ; no. 2)
    ISBN 0-945274-27-0
    1. Korean War, 1950–1953—Campaigns—Korea (South)—Inchon.
2. Korean War, 1950–1953—Amphibious operations. 3. United States.
Navy—History—20th century. 4. Inchon (Korea)—History, Military.
I. Title. II. Series.
DS918.2.I5U89 1994
951.904\2—dc20   94-34662

For sale by the U.S. Government Printing Office
Superintendent of Documents, Mail Stop: SSOP, Washington, DC 20402-9328

Foreword

This is the second study in the Naval Historical Center's monograph series, entitled "The U.S. Navy in the Modern World." The purpose of the series is to bring to the attention of today's naval personnel and other readers the contributions of the naval service to the nation, in war and peace, since 1945. During the Cold War, the Navy helped resist Communist aggression, deter nuclear and conventional attack on the United States, protect American trade at sea and ashore, strengthen regional alliances and foster the growth of democratic and free market institutions worldwide. The strength and overseas presence of the U.S. fleet often resolved crises without the use of force. But when force was necessary, the Navy fought hard and well.

In light of the Navy's current emphasis on littoral operations, I believe that *Assault from the Sea: The Amphibious Landing at Inchon*, by Curtis A. Utz of our Contemporary History Branch, is an appropriate title for the series' second work. His monograph demonstrates how the Navy's veteran leadership, flexible organization, versatile ships

and aircraft and great mobility gave the theater commander, General of the Army Douglas A. MacArthur, the ability to launch a devastating offensive against the North Korean invaders of South Korea.

In addition to the efforts of Mr. Utz, many others were involved in the production of this work. This project was skillfully supervised by Dr. Edward J. Marolda, who heads the Contemporary History Branch. As always, Dr. William S. Dudley, the center's Senior Historian, provided invaluable advice. I also wish to thank Professor Roger Dingman of the University of Southern California, a distinguished authority on the Korean War; and Brigadier General Edwin H. Simmons, USMC (Ret.), Director of Marine Corps History and Museums and an Inchon veteran, for their helpful comments and observations.

The views expressed are those of Mr. Utz alone and not those of the Department of the Navy or any other agency of the U.S. government.

Dean C. Allard
Director of Naval History

53

On the cover: "Inchon," prismacolor, by combat artist Herbert C. Hahn. This drawing depicts landing craft headed for Red Beach during the evening assault, as Inchon burns in the background. Destroyers firing in support of the landing, as well as LSTs, stand offshore. To the right is Wolmi Do and the causeway leading to Inchon.

Introduction

On 25 June 1950, the army of the Democratic People's Republic of (North) Korea stormed across the 38th parallel and invaded the Republic of (South) Korea. North Korea's Communist leader, Kim Il Sung, intended to destroy the rival government and abolish the division of Korea that resulted from international tensions after World War II. Kim launched the attack because he, and the Communist leaders in Moscow and Beijing, believed that the United States would not protect South Korea. They had made a critical mistake, however, because President Harry S. Truman roundly condemned this blatant act of aggression and persuaded the United Nations (UN) to resist the invasion. Truman also ordered U.S. ground, air and naval forces into combat in Korea. Thus began the Cold War's first major armed conflict.

Weakened by the drastic cutbacks in defense spending after World War II, the U.S. armed forces were hard pressed to delay much less stop the onrushing North Korean People's Army (NKPA). Only a small number of Navy carrier and Air Force planes were on hand to strike enemy front-line units and supply convoys. A hastily gathered and deployed Army unit made a brave, but futile stand in central South Korea. By early August, the hard-charging NKPA armored and infantry forces had pushed the U.S. Eighth Army and Republic of Korea (ROK) troops into an ever-tightening pocket around the port of Pusan on the southeastern tip of South Korea. Barring a dramatic turn of events, it looked like the U.S. and the ROK troops would be forced to evacuate the Pusan perimeter under fire, much as the British and French had done at Dunkirk in World War II.

The effort to rescue South Korea, however, was underway. General of the Army Douglas A. MacArthur, the U.S. Commander in Chief, Far East, and Commander in Chief, United Nations Command (CINCUNC), persuaded his superiors in Washington to approve an amphibious assault at Inchon, a major port 110 miles behind enemy lines on South Korea's west coast. Because of the port's treacherous waterways, he reasoned that the North Koreans would not expect an attack there, so it would be relatively poorly defended. The UN force could advance rapidly from Inchon and capture the nearby key air base at Kimpo and then mount an attack on Seoul, the capital of the Republic of Korea. Seoul was also the key link in the NKPA's line of communications and once taken would then serve as an anvil on which an Eighth Army offensive from Pusan would hammer the enemy army. The hoped-for result of this coordinated action was the complete destruction of the NKPA and the recovery of all of South Korea.

Inchon was a classic demonstration of how naval forces can be decisive in regional wars and littoral operations. During July, August and early September 1950, fleet units in the Far East established superiority in the Yellow Sea and in the air over it. The presence there of surface ships, submarines, carrier aircraft and shore-based patrol planes served to deter or, if necessary, warn the CINCUNC of Chinese or Soviet intervention in the war. Control of the sea and the air also blinded the North Koreans about UN military movements. This enabled the 230 ships of Vice Admiral Arthur D. Struble's Joint Task Force 7, which steamed toward the west coast of Korea in mid-September, to achieve a clear advantage over their foe through strategic surprise.

On 13 September 1950, Struble's forces began their assault from the sea against Inchon. Carrier-based aircraft squadrons, as well as cruisers and destroyers, devastated enemy fortifications, coastal artillery batteries and supply points for two days. Then, on the 15th, landing ships and transports began disembarking the 1st Marine Division, which quickly seized Inchon. By the 19th, the Marines captured Kimpo air base, into which flowed Marine close air support aircraft and Air Force supply transports. U.S. Army troops also pushed out from the beachhead and on the 27th linked up with their comrades advancing north from the Pusan perimeter. UN casualties were light, especially when compared to the thousands of dead, wounded and captured North Korean soldiers.

Provisioned by the Navy's transport and cargo ships, Marine, Army and South Korean troops captured Seoul on 28 September. Only a battered remnant of the NKPA was able to flee South Korea and the closing UN trap. Because of Chinese intervention in October 1950, the struggle in Korea would drag on for almost three more bloody and inconclusive years. Inchon, however, was a strategic masterstroke that clearly turned the tide of battle in the opening phase of the war.

Korea: The "Cockpit of Asia"

Korea has long been an Asian battleground. The mighty Genghis Khan and his Mongol horde swept into Korea in the 13th century. For the next 600 years, the Mongols and their successors to the throne of China dominated the diminutive Kingdom of Korea. Every year, the Korean king pledged his fealty to the emperor in Beijing, but aside from this connection with the outside world, the Koreans jealously guarded their isolation. In fact, the Korean monarchs banned overseas trade and discouraged contact between their subjects and foreigners. The ruggedness of the coastline and the perilous seas around the Korean peninsula helped enforce their royal edicts. Outsiders appropriately referred to Korea as the "Hermit Kingdom."

In the latter half of the 19th century, Americans learned just how serious the Koreans were about their desire to be left alone. In 1866, the Koreans massacred the crew of American merchant schooner *General Sherman*, which had run aground in the Taedong River near Pyongyang. The Navy dispatched Commander Robert W. Shufeldt, commanding officer of the screw sloop of war *Wachusett*, to discuss the incident with the King of Korea. The monarch refused to deal with him.

Despite this rebuff, U.S. naval leaders in the Far East convinced Washington that

NHC NH 79263

Commodore Robert Shufeldt circa 1880. As a commander, Shufeldt investigated the 1866 massacre of the crew of the American schooner *General Sherman* in Korea's Taedong River. In 1882, as a diplomatic representative of the United States, he negotiated a treaty of friendship with the King of Korea.

Korea could be "opened" for trade and diplomatic relations. The visits of Commodore Matthew C. Perry and his "black ships" to Japan in the 1850s, which stimulated the Japanese to cultivate contacts with the Western world, clearly influenced these officers. In 1871, Rear Admiral John Rodgers led five U.S. Navy warships up the Salee River until they were under the guns of the Korean forts above Inchon. The Koreans, as they had done in the past, greeted the foreigners with gunfire. Rodgers's ships returned fire and put ashore a landing party of sailors and Marines, who seized the forts.

NHC NH 79942

U.S. sailors battle Korean troops during Commodore John Rodgers attack on the forts near Inchon in 1871. Artist unknown.

3

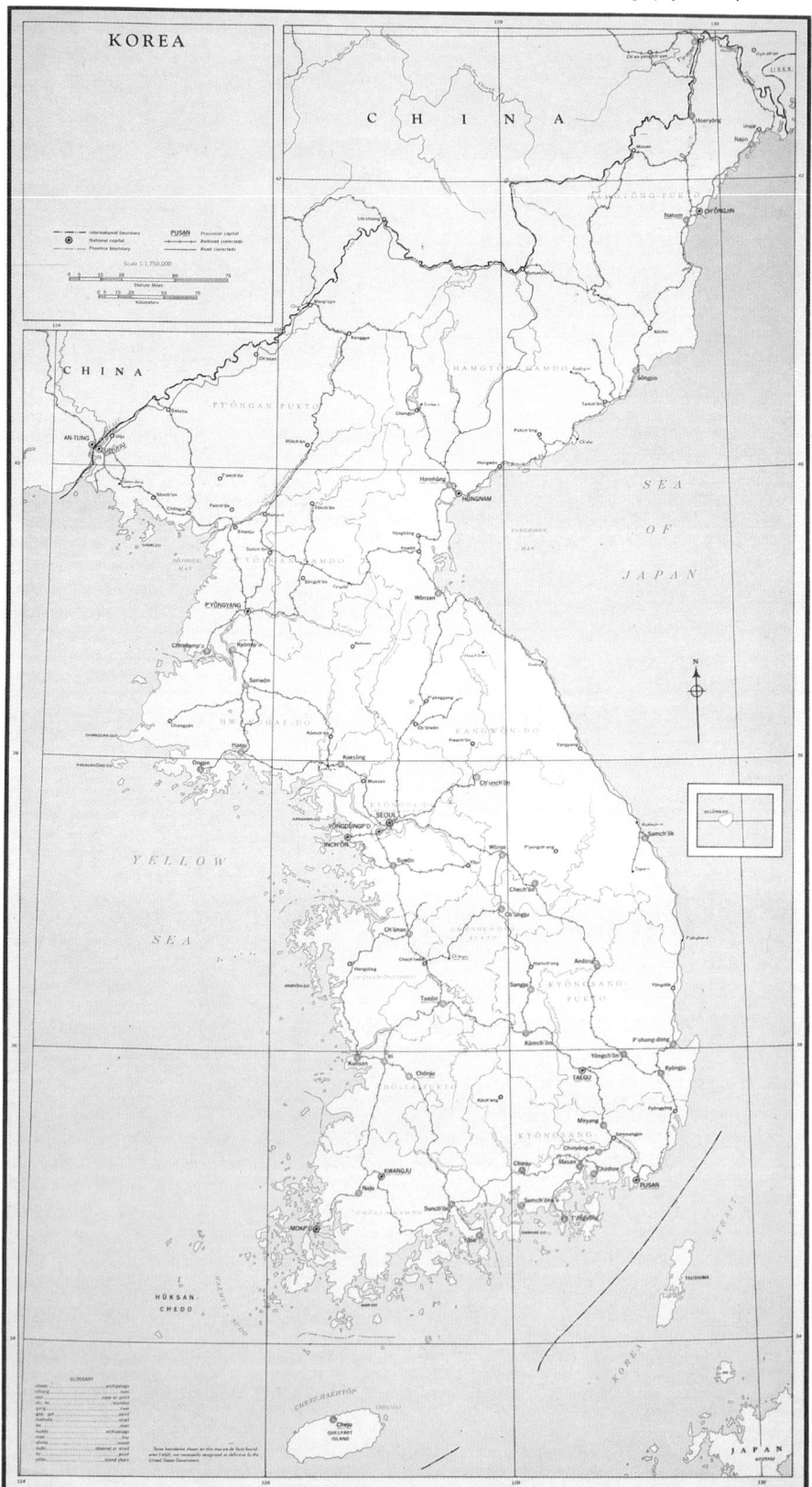

The admiral, however, did not have enough men to march on the Korean capital and impose a treaty on the king, so the Americans and their ships withdrew.

The Navy now enlisted the support of the Chinese, who encouraged the royal head of the subordinate kingdom to work with the Americans. Finally, on 22 May 1882, in sight of the U.S. screw sloop *Swatara*, Commodore Shufeldt and Korean officials signed a treaty that provided for peace, friendship and an exchange of diplomats. The agreement also granted the United States most-favored-nation treatment with special trading rights on the peninsula. The Koreans hoped this unique relationship with the United States would help fend off their more demanding neighbors, particularly the Japanese.

This proved an illusion, however, because the American interest in Korea faded even as the focus of the Chinese, Japanese and Russians sharpened. The Imperial Japanese Navy's sound thrashing of the Chinese fleet in the naval Battle of the Yalu in 1894, during the Sino-Japanese War, ended Beijing's domination of Korea. Russian designs on the kingdom met the same fate as a result of the Russo-Japanese War of 1904–1905. That conflict, fought partly on the Korean peninsula, was capped by the Japanese destruction of a Russian fleet in the Strait of Tsushima and the declaration of a "protectorate" over the country. President Theodore Roosevelt, in the interest of balancing Japanese and Russian power in Northeast Asia, endorsed Tokyo's direction of Korean affairs. Finally, in 1910, Japan formally annexed the kingdom, establishing a brutal regime that lasted until Japan's defeat by the Allied powers in 1945.

Before the end of that global conflict, Allied leaders agreed to set up a United Nations "trusteeship" over Korea, with the United States and the Soviet Union occupying Korea on either side of the 38th parallel, which was intended to be only a temporary dividing line. After disarming Japanese forces, the occupying powers planned to withdraw and re-

store Korea's independence. To carry out this mandate, in August and September 1945, Soviet and U.S. troops moved into their respective occupation zones in North and South Korea.

Ideological conflict and balance-of-power politics after

Syngman Rhee, President of the Republic of Korea. An American-educated nationalist, Rhee was a vehement anti-Communist.

World War II soon disrupted the process of Korean unification and independence. The world witnessed the dawning of the "Cold War." The United States and the other Western allies were increasingly at odds with the USSR and its ruthless dictator, Joseph Stalin. The Soviets suppressed basic freedoms and undermined governments in Poland, Czechoslovakia and the other eastern European nations that had been occupied by the Red Army. Moscow fueled an insurgency in Greece and made territorial demands on Turkey and Iran. In 1946, Mao Zedong's Chinese Communists launched an all-out campaign against Chiang Kai-shek's Nationalist government that would culminate several years later in the conquest of the entire mainland of China. The Soviet menace loomed especially large in August 1949 when the USSR detonated an atomic bomb, ending the U.S. monopoly of these weapons of mass destruction.

Meanwhile, in Korea, the Soviets supported the ascendancy of Kim Il Sung, a Communist leader whose forces had fought the Japanese in North China and Manchuria during the war. U.S. officials favored Dr. Syngman Rhee, an American-educated nationalist, and his ardent anti-Communist supporters. In both sections of the country, the Korean antagonists suppressed their opponents, often ruthlessly. Voters south of the

DoD

Kim Il Sung, leader of the People's Democratic Republic of Korea, gives a speech in 1948 with a depiction of a united Korean peninsula behind him.

38th parallel eventually elected Rhee as the first President of the Republic of Korea, formally established on 15 August 1948. The following month Kim Il Sung announced his leadership of a second political creation, the Democratic People's Republic of Korea.

During the next year and a half, the two Korean governments engaged in low-level hostilities. They sent agents, saboteurs and raiding forces across the 38th parallel and fought artillery duels along the dividing line. In the last six months of 1949 alone, there were over 400 "border incidents."

With the establishment of friendly regimes in their respective occupation zones, the USSR and the U.S. withdrew their occupation forces. The Soviet armed forces left behind a military advisory group and large amounts of World War II-vintage munitions and equipment, including tanks, artillery and combat aircraft. The North Korean armed forces continued to grow in numbers and capability under Soviet tutelage.

Except for the 500-man Korean Military Advisory Group (KMAG), the United States withdrew all of its forces from Korea by June 1949. They left behind large quantities of small arms and ammunition, but, unlike the Soviets, no tanks, medium or heavy artillery or combat aircraft. The administration

of Harry S. Truman opposed giving Rhee such "offensive" weapons, fearing that he would try to unify Korea by force. The Americans thought Rhee's new government needed only U.S. training of its armed forces, modest arms supplies and economic and political support.

The simultaneous draw down of U.S. conventional forces and reliance on military advisers and assistance reflected the Truman administration's global approach to the threat posed by the Soviet Union and its allies after World War II. In 1947, President Truman proclaimed a new strategy for dealing with the Communists' militant and expansive policies—containment. The United States and her allies would prevent the spread of Communist ideology and Soviet influence by strengthening the economies, political systems and military organizations of friendly countries. The containment strategy anticipated using U.S. ground troops, tactical aircraft units, combat fleets and other conventional forces to defend only vital national interests.

Reduced Forces

At the end of World War II, the U.S. armed forces comprised 12-million men and women who had answered the greatest call to the colors in American history. This massive establishment fielded 95 infantry, armor, airborne and Marine divisions; 92,000 aircraft; 1,307 warships; and 82,000 landing craft. But, with the war now over, the American public clamored to "bring the boys home." Operation Magic Carpet and similar movements transported millions of American soldiers, sailors, airmen and Marines home to the United States and then discharged them from the military.

Another motivation for the reduction of the military establishment was Truman's desire to improve America's financial health. Being the "Arsenal of Democracy" in World War II had been a great drain on the public treasury of the United States and had disrupted the production of consumer goods. Truman believed that it was more important to balance the budget and encourage the private sector than to buy new weapons or station large forces overseas.

Key leaders in Washington also suggested that the U.S. could reduce defense spending significantly because America had the atomic bomb. Proponents concluded that the American atomic arsenal (which was not that powerful or ready for war during the 1945–1950 period) either would deter or defeat Soviet invasions of vital areas, such as western Europe. The U.S. Air Force, separated from the Army in 1947, believed that the delivery of atomic weapons should be the mission of only its bombers. The Air Force argued that this made conventional forces, especially Navy carrier forces, much less valuable and that they should be reduced in number and capability. The Navy countered that a balanced military establishment, in which no weapon system or service predominated, best served the global interests of the United States.

All the services were involved in sometimes acrimonious disputes over dwindling budgets, their respective roles and missions in the new postwar world, and unification of the defense establishment. James V. Forrestal, the first Secretary of Defense (the National Military Establishment, later to become the Department of Defense, was established in 1947), literally worked himself to death trying to accommodate the differing views of each service. His successor, Louis V. Johnson, an incompetent political appointee with little experience in defense matters, reinforced Truman's inclination to drastically cut the defense budget. Johnson also accepted the proposition that only the Air Force should be allowed to conduct long-range atomic bombing. Without consulting the Navy's civilian or military leaders, he canceled construction of *United States* (CVA 58), the first aircraft carrier designed to carry atomic-capable aircraft. In the uproar over this and other issues, collectively called the "Revolt of the Admirals," Secretary of the Navy John L. Sullivan resigned in protest and his successor forced Admiral Louis E. Denfeld, the Chief of Naval Operations (CNO), to retire.

During the period from 1945 to 1950, all the services suffered from the loss of critical resources. The last budget approved by Congress before the outbreak of the Korean War provided for only 238 naval combatants, including 6 fleet aircraft carriers, 1 reduced-status battleship and 9 carrier air groups; 6 battalions and 12 aircraft squadrons for the Marines; and 14 reduced-strength Army divisions. Even the favored Air Force was expected to operate with 48 air groups instead of the 71 it considered essential.

The Road to War

In early 1950, international miscalculation over Korea resulted in war. For several years, Kim Il Sung had urged his Communist patrons to support a North Korean invasion of South Korea but they refused him each time. The leaders of the Soviet Union and the People's Republic of China did not want a major war to break out in northeast Asia. Stalin was more concerned about the growing strength of the North Atlantic Treaty Organization alliance in Europe. Mao Zedong was concentrat-ing his forces for the invasion of Taiwan and climactic last battle with Chiang Kai-shek's Nationalists.

The United States did not want a war in Asia, either. The Truman administration focused its attention and the combat power of the U.S. military on Europe. Truman and his Secretary of State, Dean Acheson, were determined to limit U.S. Far Eastern commitments, a desire unfortunately made public. On 12 January 1950, Acheson told the Washington press corps that the United

States would fight to defend Japan, Okinawa and the Philippines but, by failing to mention them, neither Taiwan nor Korea. So, when Kim once again asked Moscow and Beijing to approve his plans to conquer South Korea, they agreed, although Mao Zedong was somewhat reluctant. However, Mao promised to send the substantial number of ethnic Koreans in the Chinese Communist forces back to Kim.

By the late spring of 1950, the North Koreans had amassed formidable military forces. The NKPA then consisted of 135,000 men. The principal ground elements of this force were 10 infantry divisions, an armored brigade, 2 independent regiments and border constabulary troops. Two of these divisions recently had returned from China; many of the other soldiers were veterans of Mao's forces. The NKPA fielded 150 Soviet-made T-34 tanks, hundreds of light and medium artillery pieces and numerous heavy mortars. The North Korean Air Force included 70 Yakolev Yak-3 and Yak-7 fighters and 60 Ilyshin Il-10 "Shturmovik" attack planes, all propeller driven. The navy operated a few small patrol boats.

The Republic of Korea military was inferior to the NKPA in quantity and quality. The ROK Army, composed of eight infantry divisions, various support units and headquar-

Vice Admiral C. Turner Joy, Commander Naval Forces, Far East, by Navy combat artist Herbert Hahn.

ters elements, numbered only 100,000 men. They lacked good field artillery and had no tanks. The air force flew only 20 unarmed training planes. The South Korean Navy (ROKN) manned 17 old U.S. and Japanese minesweepers, a few picket boats, one tank landing ship and one subchaser, renamed *Bak Du San* (PC 701), which the U.S. Navy sold to the Koreans in 1949.

The U.S. naval forces in the western Pacific in June 1950 were a pale reflection of the mighty armada that surrounded the battleship *Missouri* (BB 63) at Tokyo Bay in September 1945. Vice Admiral Arthur D. Struble, a veteran of World War II amphibious

operations in the Philippines, commanded the Seventh Fleet, based at Subic Bay in the Philippines. In this fleet steamed fleet aircraft carrier *Valley Forge* (CV 45), heavy cruiser *Rochester* (CA 124), 8 destroyers, 4 submarines and 5 logistics support ships. Fleet Air Wing 1, with two patrol squadrons, provided the fleet with long-range search and reconnaissance aircraft. Vice Admiral C. Turner Joy, Commander Naval Forces, Japan, led a force that consisted of light cruiser *Juneau* (CLAA 119), the 4 ships of Destroyer Division 91 and the 7 minesweepers of Mine Squadron 3. Also under Admiral Joy were the five ships of Rear Admiral James H. Doyle's Amphibious Group 1. Joy was also Commander Naval Forces, Far East, and in the event of an emergency, Seventh Fleet would come under his direction, as well.

The closest American ground forces to the Korean peninsula were the four infantry divisions of Lieutenant General Walton H. Walker's Eighth Army, which served as the occupation force for Japan's Home Islands. Walker's units—the 7th, 24th and 25th Infantry Divisions and the 1st Cavalry Division (also infantry)— were in poor shape. Because of postwar defense cutbacks, these units were severely undermanned and badly equipped. Much of their material had been salvaged from World War II battlefields and restored in Japanese shops. Lacking adequate training and resources, and softened by occupation duty, the American troops in Japan were ill-prepared for war.

Manpower and material shortages also hobbled the U.S. Far East Air Force (FEAF), commanded by Lieutenant General George E. Stratemeyer. FEAF was made up of three air forces—the 20th, 13th and 5th, which operated from Okinawa and the Mariana Islands, the Philippines and Japan. FEAF operated mostly jet-powered Lockheed F-80 Shooting Stars in both the fighter and fighter-bomber roles, even though they were not well-suited to the latter mission. The only planes in FEAF designed solely for the attack role were the propeller-driven Douglas B-26 Invaders of the 3rd Bombardment Wing (Light). Also flying with FEAF were North American F-82 Twin Mustang all-weather fighters, Boeing B-29 Superfortress bombers and Douglas C-54 Skymaster transports.

While the United States could not assume it would be supported by its World War II allies in any new crisis, Australian and British forces operated in the region during early 1950. Australian occupation forces stationed in the Japanese islands were an infantry battalion, a fighter squadron equipped with North American F-51 Mustangs and the frigate HMAS *Shoalhaven* (K 535). The UN was fortunate that in June 1950 light aircraft carrier HMS *Triumph*, 2 light cruisers, 2 destroyers and 3 frigates of the Royal Navy's Far East Station were steaming toward Japan to escape the summer heat at their Southeast Asian home ports.

As U.S., Australian and British forces in the Far East carried out business as usual in the late spring of 1950, there were ominous developments on the Korean peninsula. After months of probing south across the border, in May the NKPA suddenly halted such activity. Intelligence sources in Taiwan and South Korea warned that the Communists would soon take stronger armed action. These warnings, however, fell on deaf ears. American political and military leaders believed that none of the countries interested in the Korean situation would benefit from a war on the Korean peninsula. KMAG officers told visiting American officials that all was quiet on the Korean front. On 19 June, the Central Intelligence Agency forecast that the North Koreans would continue their low-level hostilities near the 38th parallel but not launch a major attack across it that summer.

South Korean military leaders brief visiting dignitaries on the defenses at the 38th parallel on 18 June 1950. Listening intently are John Foster Dulles, President Truman's special representative and later Secretary of State; Sihn Seung Mo, the South Korean Minister of Defense; and U.S. military advisers. Few Americans or South Koreans, however, expected a North Korean invasion. One week after this photograph was taken, North Korean tanks and infantry units poured through this position.

NA 111-SC-342614

North Korean Invasion and

Early on the morning of 25 June 1950, the hills around the 38th parallel reverberated with artillery fire. This caused little alarm among the American advisers, however, because of the numerous border incidents that had occurred there during the past year. This complacency soon changed to shock as they discovered North Korean combat forces in their midst. When U.S. Army Captain Joseph R. Darrigo neared the railroad station at Kaesong, five miles south of the parallel, he discovered several NKPA battalions detraining! Overnight, the Communists had connected their rail lines to those in the south and rushed troops forward. He now knew that this was no border incident—this was an invasion!

By early afternoon, NKPA infantry and armored formations, heavily supported by aircraft and artillery, were attacking all along the border. As T-34 tanks spearheaded the main assault on Seoul, landing forces stormed ashore at several places on the east coast and outflanked ROK positions.

Some of the South Korean units fought well, but many did not. None was equipped or trained to hold off a mechanized assault. Surprised as they were, most of the ROK units disintegrated or retreated in the face of the powerful offensive. At least one South Korean unit, however, scored a victory over the attackers. After putting to sea with the few other combatants of the ROK navy, the newly arrived submarine chaser *Bak Du San* discovered a 1,000-ton armed North Korean steamer off the east coast. In a vicious surface battle, the South Koreans sank the steamer, whose 600 embarked soldiers were meant to land and seize Pusan. This proved to be one of the most important fights of the campaign for it prevented the short-term loss of this key port, soon to be vital to the survival of UN forces in Korea.

Meanwhile, chaos reigned in Seoul. With South Korean defenses around the capital crumbling, U.S. Ambassador John J. Muccio ordered the evacuation of American dependents. Protected by the destroyers *Mansfield* (DD 728) and *De Haven* (DD 727), the Norwegian freighter SS *Rheinholdt* took on the evacuees at Seoul's port, Inchon, and headed for Japan. In the next several days, Air Force transports flew other Americans and UN personnel out of nearby Kimpo and Suwon airfields. During these evacuation operations, escorting U.S. fighters shot down seven North Korean fighter and attack planes.

Even though surprised by the North Korean invasion, President Truman and his advisers in Washington took immediate action to oppose it. Truman called for an emergency meeting of the UN Security Council to consider the North Korean aggression. The council met only 23 hours after the start of the invasion and it discussed a resolution advocated by the United States that condemned the North Korean aggression, demanded an end to hostilities and called for the restoration of the 38th parallel dividing line. With the USSR's delegate absent because of an earlier dispute over the UN's failure to seat the People's

The ROK navy subchaser *Chiri San* (PC 704) sorties from San Francisco on her way to South Korea in June 1950. Her sister ship, *Bak Du San* (PC 701), engaged and sank a Communist steamer loaded with troops and headed for the critical port of Pusan on the first night of the war.

NHC NH 85490

UN Reaction

Republic of China on the Security Council, there was no Soviet veto and the council passed the resolution. Then, on the 27th, the Security Council approved a second resolution encouraging UN members to come to the armed assistance of the Republic of Korea.

Meanwhile, despite earlier uncertainty over the importance of South Korea to America's interests, Truman decided that U.S. forces should defend the country. Truman and the Joint Chiefs of Staff (JCS) were concerned that the attack on Korea was only a diversion for a major Communist offensive in Europe. Still, they ordered the combat deployment of air and naval forces in the Far East, including the Seventh Fleet, to the Korean theater.

The Seventh Fleet was important not only for the help it could provide to UN forces fighting in Korea but for its impact on North Korea's potential military allies, the People's Republic of China and the USSR. Fearing that the Communists might mount a regional offensive, Truman ordered the Seventh Fleet to "neutralize" the Taiwan Strait and then made that directive public. Truman wanted to prevent a Chinese Communist invasion of Taiwan as well as an attack on the mainland by Chiang's Nationalist forces. After steaming from Subic Bay on 27 June, the Seventh Fleet sent carrier planes flying up the Taiwan Strait as it passed close to the island on

USN 416423

Left to right: Royal Navy Captain A. D. Torlesse, Commanding Officer of HMS *Triumph*; Rear Admiral John M. Hoskins, Commander Task Force 77; Vice Admiral Arthur D. Struble, Commander Seventh Fleet; and Rear Admiral William G. Andrewes, Commander of British Commonwealth Forces, confer on board the heavy cruiser *Rochester* (CA 133), flagship of the Seventh Fleet, on 1 July 1950. As in many other 20th century conflicts, the U.S. and British navies fought side by side in Korea.

the 29th. Throughout the Korean War, Seventh Fleet forces operated along the coast of China, from the Yellow Sea in the north to Hainan in the south, discouraging the Chinese use of the sea and the air over it. Beijing later revealed that it respected the power of the fleet's air, surface and subsurface forces.

The fleet also maintained naval forces in the waters around the Soviet Far East. Shore-based patrol planes kept a close watch over Soviet air and naval bases. U.S. submarines also prowled the waters off Vladivostok and the straits from the Sea of Japan.

Meanwhile, as units of the Seventh Fleet headed for the Yellow Sea at the end of June, Admiral Joy's Naval Forces, Japan, dispatched units to Korea. Early on the 29th, cruiser *Juneau* and destroyer *De Haven* deployed

off Korea's east coast to stop Communist seaborne movement and to bombard enemy ground forces advancing down the coastal road. In the confusion during the withdrawal of South Korean forces to the south, *Juneau* tragically sank the ROKN minelayer *JML 305*, which the cruiser took for an enemy ship.

Early in July, Joy sent part of Struble's Seventh Fleet dashing into North Korean waters to hit the enemy's central nerve center, the capital at Pyongyang. Struble's Striking Force (Task Force 77), reinforced by several of Rear Admiral William G. Andrewes's Royal Navy warships, mustered 24 ships. On 3 and 4 July, only eight days after the North Korean invasion, planes from *Valley Forge* and HMS *Triumph* pounded the air base, rail yards and bridges near Pyongyang.

In addition to launching

During July and August, Pacific Fleet units streamed into the Korean theater. These included heavy cruisers *Helena* (CA 75) and *Toledo* (CA 133) and *Essex*-class carriers *Philippine Sea* (CV 47) and *Boxer* (CV 21). The latter ship brought with her from the U.S. West Coast 171 aircraft, including 146 F-51 Mustang fighters desperately needed by the Air Force. *Boxer* set a transpacific speed record, reaching Yokosuka, Japan, in only eight days. Also dispatched to Korea were the Pacific Fleet's two escort carriers, *Sicily* (CVE 118) and *Badoeng Strait* (CVE 116). *Sicily* embarked antisubmarine aircraft and 30 other fighter, attack and transport planes. *Badoeng Strait* embarked not only Marine Fighter Squadron (VMF) 214, assigned to the ship, but also the aircraft of three squadrons of Marine Aircraft Group (MAG) 33. The UN naval contingent expanded with the arrival in Korean waters of the Royal Navy's light cruiser HMS *Kenya* and British, Canadian, New Zealand, Dutch and French destroyers and frigates.

Those reinforcements soon entered the fray. On 27 July, *Toledo* shelled positions on the east coast of Korea, and on 5 August, planes from *Philippine Sea* attacked targets at Iri, Mokpo and Kunsan. Early in August, VMF-214, the "Black Sheep" squadron of World War II fame, and VMF-323, based respectively on *Sicily* and

Navy carrier and Air Force bombing attacks against the advancing North Korean forces, General MacArthur ordered Air Force transports to deploy a hastily assembled Army infantry-artillery team, Task Force Smith, to Korea. NKPA armor and infantry units overran and destroyed this brave force of 24th Infantry Division soldiers in a bloody action near Osan on 5 July.

MacArthur pleaded with the JCS for reinforcements to stop and then counterattack the invading NKPA. Since General Omar N. Bradley and the service representatives of the JCS suspected that Korea was only a Communist diversionary move, they were reluctant to dispatch a sizeable portion of the understrength U.S. armed forces to the Far East. The gravity of the UN situation in Korea and MacArthur's insistent pleas, however, soon persuaded them to grant most of the general's requests.

Naval forces answered the call for help with alacrity.

Badoeng Strait, began to strike enemy forces ashore.

UN air forces responded in similar fashion. In early July, General Stratemeyer ordered several of his Philippine-based squadrons to Japan. He also ordered that some fighter-bomber squadrons be reequipped with F-51 Mustangs stockpiled in Japan, because his F-80s experienced difficulty in the close air support role and they could not operate from the rough Korean airfields. In addition, the Air Force deployed several B-29 bomber groups to the western Pacific. The Australian F-51 squadron in Japan also joined the FEAF.

As important as naval and air forces were to the Allied defensive effort in Korea, ground forces were absolutely essential. On General MacArthur's orders, Admiral Doyle's Amphibious Group 1, Military Sea Transportation Service cargo ships and Japanese time-chartered ships

NA 80-G-417995

British destroyer HMS *Cockade* (D 34), here moored at Sasebo, Japan, in July 1950, was one of many naval units deployed to the combat theater by America's British ally.

NASM 4A 31741

Lance Corporal Bob Bell, a crew chief of No. 77 Squadron, Royal Australian Air Force, "sweats out" the safe return of his unit's F-51 Mustangs from a strike in Korea. Australian air, naval and ground forces fought well alongside their UN allies.

transported three infantry divisions (24th, 25th and 1st Cavalry) from Japan to Korea, where General Walker quickly plugged them into the front line. Only the understrength 7th Infantry Division remained in Japan. MacArthur also requested and received the infantry and artillery battalions needed to bring his Eighth

NA 80-G-418776

Aircraft carrier *Boxer* (CV 21) takes on board U.S. Air Force F-51 fighters at Naval Air Station, Alameda, California, in July 1950 for transportation to the Far East.

Army divisions up to battle strength. The JCS also ordered the U.S.-based 2nd Infantry Division, a regimental combat team (RCT) from the 11th Airborne Division, and various armor, artillery and engineer units to the Far East.

Marine combat units and Navy amphibious forces were especially critical to MacArthur's anticipated operations on the Korean peninsula. Supported by General Clifton B. Cates, Commandant of the Marine Corps, MacArthur persuaded the JCS to fully man and equip the 1st Marine Division and deploy the unit to Korea by mid-September. General Cates partially filled the understrength division with Marines pulled from bases throughout the United States, but this was not enough.

President Truman then approved Cates's request for mobilization of the entire ground element of the Marine Corps Organized Reserve and attached Navy medical units. The first contingent of the division to arrive in Korea was the 5th Marine RCT.

The amphibious ships that transported the Marine units from the United States also bolstered Admiral Doyle's amphibious force. The newcomers included three dock landing ships (LSDs), two attack transports (APAs), one tank landing ship (LST) and one medium landing ship. To complement this force, Doyle got control of LSTs operated by the Army in Japan and enlisted the assistance of the Shipping Control Administration, Japan (SCAJAP), a civilian occupation agency that controlled

Japanese merchant shipping. In the SCAJAP inventory were 34 former U.S. Navy LSTs, manned by Japanese, and Doyle quickly integrated 17 of them into his force.

Despite the growing strength of UN ground, naval and air forces, the North Korean offensive rolled on. Thin U.S. and ROK defensive lines often were broken by coordinated NKPA tank assaults and infantry flank attacks, which led to a series of demoralizing retreats. With his command in dire straits, General Walker ordered UN forces to withdraw behind the Naktong River, the last natural barrier to Pusan, on 1 August. This defensive bastion soon became known as the Pusan Perimeter.

To stiffen the ground defenses, MacArthur reinforced the Eighth Army with the

Bound for Korea, leathernecks of the 5th Marine Regiment board the attack transport *Pickaway* (APA 222) in San Diego, California, on 12 July 1950.

Tanned and sweating gunners of the Army's 64th Field Artillery Battalion operate a 105mm howitzer in defense of the Pusan Perimeter. Fighting with determination and skill, General Walker's Eighth Army units defeated one NKPA attack after another during the brutally hot summer of 1950.

Men of the 5th Marine Regiment withstand an enemy mortar barrage on 3 September as they defend the high ground near the hotly contested Naktong Bulge. Less than two weeks later, these Marines would storm ashore at Inchon.

NA 127-GK-234K-A-2231

USN 417110

Captain John S. Thach, a highly decorated World War II veteran and originator of the "Thach Weave" fighter tactic, and commanding officer of the escort carrier *Sicily* (CVE 118) discusses a mission with two of his pilots, 1st Lieutenant Roland B. Heilman (left) and Major Robert P. Keller of VMF-214. Marine fighter squadrons operating from *Sicily* and *Badoeng Strait* (CVE 116) flew hundreds of ground support sorties during August 1950.

USN 421462

The eight-inch guns of heavy cruiser *Helena* (CA 75) bombard Communist forces ashore. Throughout the summer of 1950, cruisers and destroyers rained thousands of shells on enemy troops, armored vehicles and supply trucks all along the coast of South Korea.

2nd Infantry Division and the Marine Brigade, comprised of the 5th Marine RCT and MAG-33. During the first two weeks of August, the NKPA launched four major attacks. The Marine Brigade repelled two of them, including a serious penetration in the vital "Naktong Bulge" sector. Navy cruisers and destroyers provided gunfire support that helped repel assaults near the coast, as well. In early September, the Marine Brigade countered one last NKPA breakthrough at the Naktong Bulge.

Throughout this period, U.S. Air Force, Navy and Marine, as well as British and Australian, planes struck targets throughout Korea. Navy Underwater Demolition Team (UDT) and Marine reconnaissance detachments executed raids ashore from the high-speed transport *Horace A. Bass* (APD 124). By 4 September, Communist forces were spent. There would be no more major attacks on the perimeter, but MacArthur expected the NKPA to be just as tough on the defense as it had been on the offense. The general had no intention of launching the Eighth Army on a frontal assault against the dogged North Koreans.

Counterstroke

MacArthur, the veteran commander of numerous littoral operations in the southwest Pacific during World War II, was quick to see the strategic possibilities offered by the Korean peninsula. Less than one week after Kim Il Sung's Communist legions poured across the 38th parallel into the Republic of Korea, CINCUNC began to consider how he could defeat his landbound adversary. MacArthur's visit to the Korean battlefield on 29 June convinced him that the NKPA would push the underequipped, battered and demoralized ROK army, even if bolstered by U.S. reinforcements, far to the south of Seoul. MacArthur felt that his forces could turn the tables on the enemy by exploiting one key advantage over them—strategic mobility. He decided that a decisive stroke, an amphibious assault somewhere behind NKPA lines, could liberate South Korea.

MacArthur concluded that his enemy was most vulnerable to a landing on Korea's west coast at Inchon. Capture of this sizeable port and the nearby air base at Kimpo would enable the UN to mount a major attack on Seoul, not only the capital of South Korea but the key road and rail link in the NKPA's line of communications. A northwestward UN offensive from the Pusan Perimeter would then push across the peninsula, trapping most of the enemy army in the south. The U.S. divisions from the perimeter would also link up with the units at Inchon. The isolated NKPA formations would be forced to surrender or be crushed between the UN forces. Success at Inchon could lead to a glorious, one-stroke UN victory in the war, a prospect the gifted but vain MacArthur could only relish.

MacArthur Sells Inchon

MacArthur selected the small Joint Strategic Plans and Operations Group (JSPOG) of his Far East Command (FECOM) staff to bring his concept to fruition. The general's advocacy of an amphibious operation sometime before October and selection of Inchon as the site were, according to Admiral Struble, the general's "earliest and most important" decisions.

Planners were free to concentrate on overcoming the Inchon site's difficulties, and they were serious, indeed. In the words of Lieutenant Commander Arlie G. Capps, Admiral Doyle's gunnery officer, "We drew up a list of every natural and geographic handicap—and Inchon had 'em all." The approaches from the Yellow Sea were two restricted passages, Flying Fish and Eastern channels, and they joined at Palmi Do island. Palmi Do stood at the end of the narrow Salee River, 10 miles downstream from Inchon. Both channels and the Salee could be easily blocked by mines. In addition, the normal harbor current at Inchon was a dangerously quick two to three knots and sometimes even eight knots. The anchorage was small, there were few docks and piers and no landing beaches—in the usual meaning of that term—only sea walls, piers, salt pans and "rocks with patches of sand." Just offshore, a triangular-shaped island, Wolmi Do, and an islet, Sowolmi Do, separated the city from the Salee River.

Several heights dominated the landing area. The 315-foot-high Radio Hill on Wolmi Do completely commanded the harbor. Presenting a sheer cliff to the harbor side and rising to 102 feet, Cemetery Hill guarded the 800-yard-long causeway that led to Wolmi Do. Observatory Hill, 238 feet high, and the smaller British Consulate Hill overlooked the city itself.

Perhaps the most critical factor was Inchon's extreme tidal range of 32 feet, which limited a daylight landing to three or four days each

General of the Army Douglas A. MacArthur grasps the arms of Army Chief of Staff General J. Lawton Collins (left) and Chief of Naval Operations Admiral Forrest P. Sherman on their arrival at Tokyo airfield on 21 August 1950. Two days later, MacArthur turned in a masterful performance to persuade his guests that the proposed amphibious assault at Inchon would succeed.

month. Tidal waters had to be high enough to cover the wide mud flats that fronted the city. Since the highest tides in September occurred in mid-month, the JSPOG selected 15 September as D day. FECOM had less than two months to plan an assault that normally took three to five months of work. Nonetheless, MacArthur's headquarters issued Operation Plan 100-B, code-named "Chromite," with Inchon as the objective.

Doyle and many of the officers on the staff were concerned that Inchon might be too risky, so they investigated alternative sites. Doyle dispatched *Horace A. Bass* and her UDT/Marine team to scout Kunsan, which they found to be better suited to an amphibious assault. The JSPOG prepared a plan for a Kunsan operation, just in case MacArthur changed his mind on the attack site.

Although commanders in the Far East understood the difficulties of the proposed assault, the JCS was "somewhat in the dark." On 20 August, Admiral Forrest P. Sherman, the CNO; General J. Lawton Collins, the Army Chief of Staff; and other high-ranking officers flew from Washington to MacArthur's Tokyo headquarters for a briefing on the planned amphibious operation in Korea.

Admiral Doyle's staff sum-

This detailed map of the Inchon area, prepared in 1950, clearly shows the narrow passages and numerous mud and tidal flats in the approaches to the harbor.

marized the details of the assault: weather, hydrography, landing craft, beaches, naval gunfire and air support. Intelligence on the enemy forces at Inchon suggested that only a few weak units operated there and that the harbor's defenses were not completed. Doyle, a veteran of Guadalcanal and other World War II landings, ended the briefing with the statement that "the best I can say is that Inchon is not impossible." This reinforced the misgivings already felt by some of the assembled offi-cers, so they asked probing questions about alternative landing sites such as Kunsan.

MacArthur, at that time revered by many Americans as a military genius and legendary hero, slowly rose to address the assembled officers. In his well-known theatrical style and sonorous voice, the general spent the next 45 minutes delivering an oration that awed his audience. MacArthur never swayed from his choice of Inchon as the landing site. He observed that because the conditions at Inchon were so difficult, the enemy would not expect a landing there. Success at Inchon could end the war, while a seizure of Kunsan or another alternative site would be indecisive and lead to a brutal winter campaign. Looking at Admiral Sherman, the general spoke with conviction: "The Navy has never let me down in the past and it will not let me down this time." Concluding this masterful performance, MacArthur quietly but forcefully stated that "we shall land at Inchon and I shall crush them!"

Preparing for Operation Chromite

When Sherman and Collins returned to Washington, the JCS formally approved MacArthur's intention to assault Inchon on 15 September, and this spurred FECOM's preparation effort. MacArthur's greatest concern was the availability and readiness of ground troops for Chromite. Many of the forces that he hoped to hold in reserve for the amphibious assault at Inchon had been thrown into battle on the Naktong or would arrive in the theater late. The 5th Marine RCT of his primary assault force, the 1st Marine Division, spent much of August and early September fending off NKPA thrusts into the Pusan Perimeter.

The unit had only eight days to rest from combat, prepare for the amphibious operation and embark for the passage to Inchon. The division's third regiment would not arrive in the Far East until two days after the landing. When MacArthur ordered the 2nd Infantry Division, his first choice for the Army component, to the front in Korea, he had to replace it with Major General David G. Barr's half-strength 7th Infantry Division based in Japan. The Army channeled to Barr's division all arriving replacement personnel, including experienced non-commissioned officers from the schools at Fort Benning, Georgia, and Fort Sill, Oklahoma. This was still not enough, so MacArthur authorized the division to incorporate over 8,000 Korean troops, called KATUSAs (Korean Augmentation to the U.S. Army). Finally, for lack of alternatives, the American planners were compelled to use the understrength, ill-equipped—but enthusiastic—1st Korean Marine Corps (KMC) Regiment as the reserve contingent and Inchon mop-up unit.

Doyle's staff focused their efforts on the operational aspects of Chromite. They decided that amphibious ships and craft would approach Inchon by way of Flying Fish Channel, which was a rougher seaway than Eastern Channel but less subject to enemy artillery fire. Two days prior to the landing, cruisers and destroyers would steam into the harbor to shell Wolmi Do and check the waters for mines.

Even though the Japanese and American tide tables did not agree, planners estimated that high tides would occur shortly after sunrise and then just after sunset on 15 September. Since most of the amphibious ships would need daylight to navigate the narrow, swift waters of Flying Fish Channel and the Salee River, the planners decided that the smaller initial landing would take place on the morning tide. A reinforced Marine battalion would storm ashore at Green Beach on Wolmi Do and seize this island that dominated the harbor. With close air and naval gunfire support, the unit was expected to hold off any North Korean counterattacks during the day. The main assault would occur as the tide rose in the evening. Two Marine battalions would land at Red Beach, just north of the causeway from Wolmi Do, and seize the three hills in town. An entire Marine regiment would land at Blue Beach, three miles to the south of Red Beach.

Both "beaches" were in actuality built-up industrial areas largely bounded by sea walls. Vehicle and personnel landing craft (LCVP) and medium landing craft (LCM) were responsible for deploying the leathernecks to shore at Red Beach. Tracked landing vehicles (LVT), also known as amtracs, would transport the Marines in the first waves at Blue Beach, because the approach crossed two miles of mud flats covered by shallow water. LCVPs would bring in the rest of the regiment in later waves. Navy and Marine planners concluded that both beachheads were defensible, even though separated by the built-up section of Inchon.

The planners paid special attention to logistics support, which would be vital to the success of not only the initial assault on Inchon but the breakout to Seoul. They knew that the existing port facilities were rudimentary and even those would probably be destroyed in combat. Initially, all material would have to be moved across the beach. In addition, the narrow approaches from the sea would allow only a few ships at a time to operate off Inchon.

The Navy's LSTs, which were designed to operate in shallow water and unload cargo directly onto the beach, were key to success at Inchon. Doyle assembled 17 U.S. Navy LSTs and 30 Japanese-manned SCAJAP vessels. The admiral, understanding the importance of keeping the Marines supplied with ammunition and equipment in the early, critical stage of the landing, planned to leave some of his LSTs aground as the evening tide receded. They would be replaced by other ships with the following morning's tide. Hence, the LSTs, which in World War II were often referred to by their crews as "large, slow targets," would in this instance be "large, stationary targets."

The planners knew that accurate intelligence was critical to the success of an operation as complex as an amphibious assault. Consequently, in late August, the FECOM acted to gather more information about the waterways leading to Inchon. On 19 August, the Canadian destroyer HMCS *Athabaskan* (DDE 219) escorted a ROK navy vessel to Yonghung Do, an island only 14 miles from Inchon. Lieutenant Commander Ham Myong Su led a small team ashore where they found the inhabitants sympathetic to the South Korean cause. Armed with this information, on 1 September FECOM dispatched to the island Navy Lieutenant Eugene F. Clark, a former LST skipper. Under the noses of nearby NKPA island garrisons, Clark's team gathered information on surrounding waterways. The lieutenant informed Tokyo that the Japanese tide tables were accurate, the area's mud flats would support no weight, sea walls were higher than estimated and Wolmi Do was heavily fortified and bristled with numerous artillery pieces. Clark reported that even though the Canadians had disabled Palmi Do lighthouse, it was easily repairable. Tokyo told the intrepid officer to relight the beacon just after midnight on 15 September.

The "Blackbeard of Yonghung Do"

Accurate intelligence of Inchon and its water approaches was absolutely vital to the success of Operation Chromite, and no one did more to provide that information than Lieutenant Eugene F. Clark, a daring and resourceful naval officer.

The staffs planning Chromite needed detailed information on the Inchon harbor, the local tides, the waterways leading to the port and enemy defenses. While UN forces fought to hold the Pusan Perimeter, South Korean naval forces raided the peninsula's west coast and occupied Yonghung Do, an island only 14 miles from Inchon.

Far East Command decided to dispatch a reconnaissance team to the island under Lieutenant Clark. This 16-year veteran had joined the Navy as an enlisted man, earned a commission and commanded an LST and a transport after World War II. Because Clark knew that Inchon was the actual site of the forthcoming UN invasion, he decided he would kill himself rather than divulge that information if captured by the enemy. During the operation, the lieutenant carried a grenade with him everywhere because he believed it to be "more certain than . . . a pistol."

His small team included two South Korean interpreters, both of whom had served as officers in the Japanese military during World War II, and an individual identified in one account as a "U.S. Army major" but who may have been a member of a U.S. intelligence agency.

Clark's team landed on Yonghung Do on 1 September and quickly organized a force of local men and boys to keep watch on the nearby enemy-held island of Taebu Do. As a gesture of good will, Clark dispensed rice and dried fish to the islanders. Clark, who later said he felt like Blackbeard the pirate, equipped Yonghung Do's one motorized sampan with a .50-caliber machine gun and armed his men with carbines and submachine guns. To acquire information about the enemy, the team seized local fishing sampans—interrogating crewmen who generally professed loyalty to South Korea—and explored Inchon harbor. Clark's young Korean comrades also infiltrated Inchon, Kimpo air base and even Seoul and returned with valuable intelligence.

Clark informed Tokyo that the Japanese-prepared tide tables were accurate, that the mud flats fronting Inchon would support no weight and that the harbor's sea walls were higher than estimated. Clark also reported that Wolmi Do was heavily fortified and studded with Soviet-made artillery pieces. Grateful naval planners incorporated these facts into the landing plan.

The North Koreans were aware of Clark's presence on Yonghung Do, but they sent only small parties to the island to investigate. On 7 September, however, two days after several British ships bombarded Inchon, the enemy sent one motorized and three sailing sampans loaded with troops to Clark's hideaway. South Korean

A Time of Deception and

As important as it was to provide friendly forces with current intelligence, it was absolutely vital to deny the enemy information on the UN landing site. Without the element of surprise, the Marines, sailors and soldiers might find a heavily armed and dug-in enemy waiting for them at Inchon.

To prevent such a catastrophe, MacArthur's command

Lieutenant Eugene F. Clark, standing at the far right, on Yonghung Do. Pictured with him are his interpreters, several of his young followers and, probably, a South Korean navy officer.

lookouts spotted the approaching boats, so Clark and his men got their "flagship" underway. As the antagonists closed on one another, a 37-millimeter anti-tank gun mounted in the bow of the Communist motorized craft opened up. A shell splashed well in front of Clark's sampan. Undeterred by this poor shooting, and in "Nelsonian style," Clark directed his flagship to close to within 100 yards of the enemy squadron. His .50-caliber machine gun raked two of the North Korean vessels, sinking one and demolishing another. Witnessing this slaughter, the remaining boats fled the scene.

After Clark reported this engagement to headquarters, the destroyer *Hanson* (DD 832) showed up to take off the team. Clark, who had not asked to be extracted, instead requested *Hanson*'s skipper to pound Taebu Do. *Hanson* blasted the island with 212 five-inch rounds, and Marine Corsairs covering the destroyer also bombed and strafed the North Korean lair.

The team stayed on the island and continued their mission. Clark scouted Palmi Do, an island centrally located in the approaches to Inchon, and reported that Canadian raiders had only damaged the lighthouse beacon. Tokyo ordered Clark to relight the lamp at midnight on the 15th. On 14 September, Clark's team left Yonghung Do for Palmi Do and repaired the light.

Meanwhile, the North Korean commander at Inchon sent a contingent to wipe out the bothersome force on Yonghung Do. At dusk on the 14th, the enemy troops crossed the mud flats from Taebu Do to Yonghung Do. The Communists overwhelmed the island defenders and executed over 50 men, women and children.

Clark avenged their sacrifice for the UN cause when he activated the beacon atop the lighthouse at midnight on 15 September. With this light to guide them, the ships of the Advance Attack Group safely threaded their way through the treacherous approach to Inchon.

In recognition of his heroic work off Inchon, the Navy awarded Lieutenant Eugene F. Clark the Silver Star and the Army presented him with the Legion of Merit.

Uncertainty

staged an elaborate deception operation. The purpose was to encourage the North Koreans to believe the landing would occur at Kunsan, 105 miles south of Inchon. FEAF bombers began isolating Kunsan on 5 September by bombing roadways and

Air Force Douglas B-26 Invaders of the 3rd Bomb Group (Light) fire rockets at boxcars and other targets in the rail yard at Iri, near Kunsan. Attacks like this one were intended to deceive the North Koreans about the true site of the forthcoming allied amphibious landing.

bridges leading to the port. On 6 September, Admiral Andrewes's cruisers and destroyers bombarded Kunsan, a day after shelling Inchon. During early September, planes from HMS *Triumph* and *Badoeng Strait* hit railroads and bridges from Kunsan north to Pyongyang. Meanwhile, ROK navy small boats raided enemy positions along the west coast. Disinformation was also part of

the deception effort. On a Pusan dock, Marine officers briefed their men about the landing beaches at Kunsan despite the numerous Koreans within earshot.

As the actual landing date came closer, activity near Kunsan increased. In addition to the regular FEAF attacks, on 11 September B-29 bombers struck Kunsan's military installations. During the night of 12–13 September,

"Scratch One," by Navy combat artist Herbert Hahn, depicts carrier planes dropping bridge spans in the campaign to deny enemy front-line units supplies and reinforcements.

the British frigate HMS *Whitesand Bay* (F 633) landed U.S. Army special operations troops and Royal Marine Commandos on the docks, who made sure the enemy knew of their short presence ashore.

FECOM worked even harder to keep the true destination of Admiral Struble's task force secret. With men, supplies and ships concentrating in the ports of Japan and at Pusan, there was no way to hide the fact that an amphibious operation was about to take place. So widespread was the speculation that the press in Japan referred to the impending landing as "Operation Common Knowledge." Confirming MacArthur's worst fears, in early September, counterintelligence agents uncovered a North Korean–Japanese spy ring. When the leader of the ring was arrested, he had a copy of the Chromite operation plan. No one knew if he had been able to transmit the plan to Pyongyang.

Not only were UN commanders uncertain about how the North Koreans would react to an amphibious assault, but also how the Chinese and Soviets would respond. Communist ships and aircraft operated from bases that were only 100 miles from UN fleet units in the Yellow Sea. The 80 submarines of the Soviet Pacific Ocean Fleet at Vladivostok also posed a potential threat. U.S. submarines, surface ships and patrol aircraft, based on shore and afloat, maintained a constant watch in the Yellow Sea and the Sea of Japan to detect any hostile activities.

Anxiety rose on 4 September when the radar picket destroyer *Herbert J. Thomas* (DDR 833) picked up an unidentified aircraft contact heading from Port Arthur in Manchuria toward the UN task force in the Yellow Sea. Air controllers vectored a flight of four Fighter Squadron 53 Vought F4U Corsairs from the combat air patrol toward the intruder. Thirty miles north of Task Force 77, the Corsair pilots saw one twin-engined plane dive and head for Korea. The flight leader, Lieutenant (jg) Richard E. Downs, closed on the suspicious aircraft. It was an American-made Douglas A-20 Havoc light bomber, many of which were provided to the USSR in the World War II lend-lease program. The A-20, emblazoned with the red star of the Soviet air force, suddenly fired at Downs. After receiving permission from *Valley Forge*, Downs opened up on the "hostile." Downs overshot the target, but his wingman riddled the bomber and sent it slamming into the ocean. When crewmen from *Herbert J. Thomas* recovered the pilot's body, they confirmed that he was a Russian. Leaders in Washington and Tokyo wondered if this event presaged Soviet and possibly Chinese intervention in the war.

Into the Gale

Soon after the ships of Admiral Doyle's amphibious armada put to sea from the ports of Kobe and Yokohama, Japan, they faced age-old enemies, howling winds and raging waters. Navy weather planes and aerologists had warned Doyle days earlier that Typhoon Kezia was headed his way, which caused him to speed up the fleet's loading and departure process. Hard work on the docks and on board the ships allowed the task force to sortie by 11 September, one day ahead of schedule. Doyle's flagship, *Mount McKinley* (AGC 7), already being pounded by the rising swell, was the last vessel to leave Kobe. Still, on the 12th, Kezia battered the fleet with 90-knot winds and massive waves. Doyle later described it as the worst storm he ever experienced.

The tempest sorely tested the ships and sailors of the flotilla. After losing her port engine, *LST 1048* had to fight to maintain steerageway. The salvage ship *Conserver* (ARS 39) came alongside the struggling landing ship and floated down a hawser. Working on a wet, pitching deck, the LST's sea and anchor detail chocked the line into place and soon had secured a towing cable passed by *Conserver*. While only making six knots, the two ships proceeded together and reached Inchon on time for the fight.

On 12 September, Captain Norman Sears's Advance Attack Group and three attack

Navy Art Collection, KN 19250

The ships of Task Force 90 faced perilous seas, such as those depicted in Herbert Hahn's "Heavy Weather," as they fought to make way during Typhoon Kezia.

transports stood out of Pusan with the 5th Marines embarked. After a second Naktong Bulge battle, the regiment barely had time to refit and integrate reinforcements from the United States. Before leaving Pusan, Marine leaders selected Lieutenant Colonel Robert D. Taplett's 3rd Battalion, 5th Marines, to make the initial assault on Wolmi Do.

Meanwhile, Doyle's *Mount McKinley* steered for Sasebo, Japan. There, MacArthur

Fast transport *Wantuck* (APD 125) and dock landing ship *Comstock* (LSD 19), loaded with Marines and their equipment, shape a course for Inchon.

NA 80-G-423221

came on board with his entourage, which included ten of the general's favorite journalists, all of whom Doyle later quipped "wanted to travel in the light of the sun." They joined Major General Edward M. Almond, Commander X Corps; Lieutenant General Lemuel C. Shepherd, Commander Fleet Marine Force, Pacific; and Major General Oliver P. Smith, Commander 1st Marine Division, and their respective staffs, all of them cramped in one relatively small ship.

By 14 September, the entire invasion force was headed for the Yellow Sea and Inchon. Admiral Struble's Joint Task Force 7 comprised forces from 9 nations, including 230 warships, amphibious ships and auxiliaries; the 1st Marine Division and the 7th Infantry Division; 21 aircraft squadrons; and special amphibious, engineer, logistics and UDT units. His subordinate, Admiral Doyle, was responsible for executing the actual assault and getting the Marine and Army troops ashore.

As laid out in Joint Task Force 7 Operations Plan 9-50, Struble divided his command into six components. The aircraft of the Fast Carrier Force (Task Force 77) flew fighter cover, interdiction and ground attack missions. Admiral Andrewes's Blockade and Covering Force (Task Force 91) carried out pre-landing deception operations with naval gunfire and air strikes, protected the amphibious force from surface and air threats and patrolled the waters off the west coast of Korea. The patrol squadrons and seaplane tenders of Rear Admiral George R. Henderson's Patrol and Reconnaissance Force (Task Force 99) stood ready to provide aerial escort for the transports and search the surrounding waters. Logistics support was the responsibility of Captain Bernard L. Austin's Service Squadron 3 (Task Force 79).

As detailed in Amphibious Group 1 Operation Order 14-50, Doyle led the major invasion element, the Attack Force (Task Force 90). This formation included all the amphibious and transport ships, a gunfire support group and the escort carriers embarking Marine air squadrons. Additional Navy transports, Military Sea Transportation Service ships and chartered merchantmen would start bringing in the 7th Division on 18 September. Once a beachhead was established, Almond would take charge of forces ashore and direct their push toward Seoul and the UN forces advancing north from Pusan.

"Ten Enemy Vessels Approaching"

On the morning of 13 September, Rear Admiral John M. Higgins's gunfire support ships steamed up the narrow channel toward Inchon. At 1010, during the day's first flood tide, destroyers *Mansfield*, *De Haven*, *Lyman K. Swenson* (DD 729), *Collett* (DD 730), *Gurke* (DD 783) and *Henderson* (DD 785), followed by cruisers *Rochester*, *Toledo*, HMS *Jamaica* and HMS *Kenya*, entered the outer harbor. Aware that one disabled ship could block the vital channel, destroyer officers had their boatswain's mates rig towing gear to quickly pull a damaged or grounded ship out of the way. Repair parties, armed with Browning automatic rifles, carbines and submachine guns, stood by to repel enemy boarders who might attack from nearby sampans or the mud flats. Overhead, a combat air patrol of Task Force 77 Grumman F9F Panther jets provided cover.

At 1145, a lookout on *Mansfield* cried out, "Mines!" Commander Oscar B. Lundgren, *De Haven*'s commanding officer and a mine warfare expert, spied the menacing black shapes of 17 contact mines. The three leading destroyers fired on the mines with their 20mm and 40mm guns, plus small arms. A thunderous explosion tore through the air and a plume of muddy water leapt

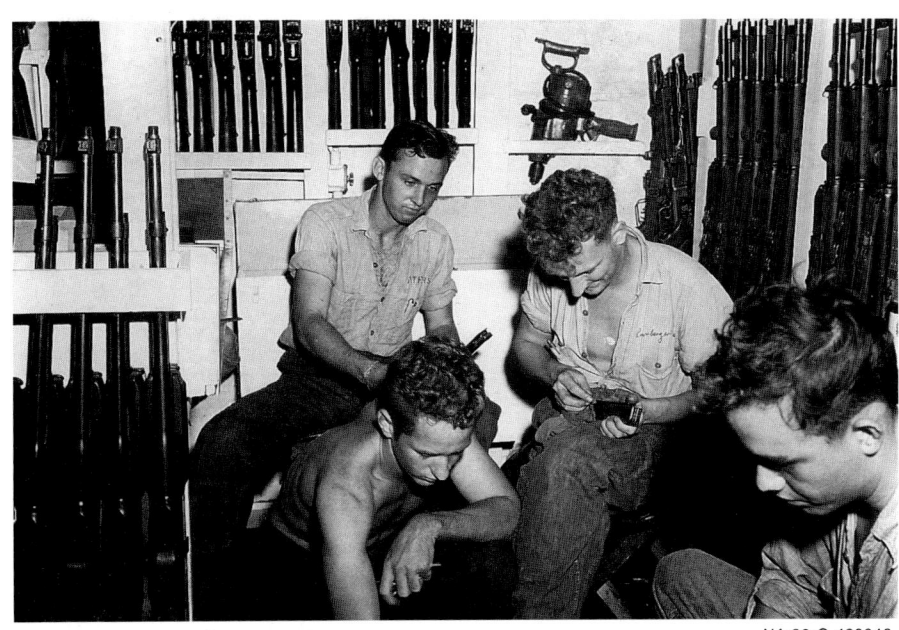

As many American bluejackets before them in the 200-year history of the U.S. Navy, these *Lyman K. Swenson* (DD 729) sailors—(left to right) Fire Control Seaman Byron M. Waters and Seamen Lavon Shaw, Warren F. Rosenberger and Rodolfo Rodreguez—prepare weapons to repel boarders as the destroyer approaches Inchon.

NA 80-G-420046

skyward as one mine exploded. Captain Halle C. Allen, Commander Destroyer Squadron 9, ordered *Henderson* to stay behind and eliminate the remaining mines. Soon afterward, the destroyer sailors discovered, from the piles of Soviet-made mines they spied ashore, that the enemy was in the process of completely mining the water approaches to Inchon.

As the ships moved to

their firing positions, propeller-driven Douglas AD Skyraiders from *Philippine Sea* blasted Wolmi Do with bombs, rockets and gunfire. The cruisers remained in the outer harbor, while the destroyers dropped anchor above and below the island. The destroyers swung on their anchors on the incoming tide, bows downstream, prepared to exit quickly, if necessary. The gunners loaded their five-inch guns, trained them to port and located their assigned targets.

"Ten enemy vessels approaching Inchon," the North Korean commander radioed in the clear to NKPA headquarters in Pyongyang. He added, "Many aircraft are bombing Wolmi Do. There is every indication that the enemy will perform a landing." The Communist officer assured his superiors that his defense force was prepared for action and would throw the enemy back into the sea.

In *De Haven*'s gun director, Lieutenant Arthur T. White saw North Korean soldiers run out and load a gun just north of Red Beach. White requested permission to open fire and Lundgren gave it. *De Haven*'s fire, which quickly eliminated the enemy weapon, proved to be the opening salvo of the prelanding bombardment.

The object of this effort

The after turret on *Toledo* (CA 133) fires a salvo of eight-inch rounds at targets near Inchon during the preinvasion bombardment.

NA 80-G-419913

was to stimulate the enemy guns in Inchon and emplaced on Wolmi Do to return fire so the UN ships could target and destroy them. For a long eight minutes, the North Koreans failed to rise to the bait. But then the defenders, men of the 918th Coastal Artillery Regiment, wheeled out their weapons—mainly Soviet-made 76mm anti-tank guns—and opened fire, hitting *Collett* seven times, *Gurke* three. The response was devastating. The gunfire support ships poured 998 five-inch rounds into the island and defenses in front of the city. At 1347, with many enemy guns silenced, Allen signaled the retirement order to his destroyers, which headed for the open sea. The cruisers provided covering fire for this movement and then brought up the rear of the column.

Before the ships could clear the harbor, however, one of the few remaining Communist guns exacted revenge on *Lyman K. Swenson*. Two North Korean shells exploded just off the destroyer's port side, killing Lieutenant (jg) David H. Swenson, ironically the nephew of the sailor for whom the ship was named. Enemy fire wounded another eight men in the bombardment force that day.

That night Higgins and Allen conferred with Struble in *Rochester*. Although pleased with the day's action, Struble ordered the ships and aircraft to give Wolmi Do "a real working-over" the following day. The mine threat remained because gunfire had eliminated only three of the devices and the task force minesweepers were several hundred miles away from Inchon. Because of the lack of small combatants, the minesweepers had been assigned to troop transport escort duty. Struble now ordered the ships to make best speed to the operational area, even though they would not arrive until 15 September. Soon after midnight the admiral dismissed his officers so they could grab a few hours of sleep and prepare for the next day's combat.

The following morning, the ships of the bombardment group hove to, with colors at half-mast and crews at quarters. A boatswain's mate in *Toledo* piped "All hands to bury the dead." After a simple service, a Marine rifle salute and the playing of "Taps," bluejackets committed Lieutenant (jg) Swenson's remains to the deep. Somber but determined after this ceremony, the men of the cruiser-destroyer group again prepared for action.

The ships once again moved up Flying Fish Channel. As the force closed Inchon, *Toledo* fired on one mine, exploding it. The damaged *Collett* dropped off and destroyed another five of the deadly "weapons that wait."

At 1116, when they came in range of targets ashore, the cruisers loosed a salvo.

NA 80-G-420889

North Korean guns emplaced ashore returned the fire of the Allied surface ships, sometimes with telling effect. (Left to right) Pipefitter 3rd Class George Broome, Seaman Apprentice Edgar O. Smith and Engineman 1st Class David L. Bollingham pose with a hole blown in the destroyer *Collett* (DD 730) by a Communist 76mm gun.

Rear Admiral James H. Doyle, Commander Task Force 90; Vice Admiral Arthur D. Struble, Commander Joint Task Force 7; and Rear Admiral John M. Higgins, Commander Task Group 90.6, confer on board Struble's flagship, heavy cruiser *Rochester* (CA 124), on 13 September 1950.

the offending guns. In the next 75 minutes, the destroyers hurled over 1,700 five-inch shells into Wolmi Do. The cruisers reentered the fray and as Marine and British Fleet Air Arm pilots spotted targets, they blasted positions near Inchon and on Wolmi Do. One *Valley Forge* pilot observed that "the whole island," referring to the once-wooded Wolmi Do, "looked like it had been shaved."

The Advance Attack Group, then in the Yellow Sea, stood in toward Flying Fish Channel. Near dusk and sixty-five miles from the objective, Commander Clarence T. Doss, Jr., in charge of three rocket bombardment ships (LSMRs), spied a huge pillar of smoke on the horizon to the east. Doss knew this meant that UN ships and planes were plastering the enemy defenders. He passed that "welcome news" to all hands.

NA 80-G-420016

Sailors prepare to commit the body of Lieutenant (jg) David Swenson to the deep on the morning of 14 September. Ironically, Swenson, the first naval officer killed in action at Inchon, was the nephew of Captain Lyman K. Swenson, for whom the destroyer in the background was named.

NKPA gunners then opened up on HMS *Kenya*, the closest cruiser to shore. Captain Patrick W. Brock, RN, *Kenya*'s skipper, felt that "the enemy gunners were either very brave or very stupid," be-cause even before the cruiser could return fire, attack aircraft obliterated

Naval gunfire from heavy cruiser *Toledo* (CA 133) explodes a Soviet-made sea mine in the approaches to Inchon on 14 September. If the enemy had had more time to lay mines off Inchon, the result might have been disastrous to the operation.

NA 80-G-419911

"Land the Landing Force"

Just after midnight on D day, 15 September, the Advance Attack Group and the bombardment group formed into an 18-ship column and entered Flying Fish Channel. Two hours later, lookouts in the lead ships noticed a rhythmically flashing light in the darkness ahead of them. The rotating beacon atop the Palmi Do lighthouse guided each ship safely through the narrow passage. Lieutenant Clark, who had activated the light, shivered in his lofty perch not only from the chilly night air but from the thrill of seeing the fleet steaming into Inchon.

At 0508, *Mount McKinley* dropped anchor in the channel and the gunfire support ships and amphibious vessels moved to their assigned positions. At 0520, Doyle hoisted the traditional signal that had preceded many amphibious assaults in naval history: "Land the landing force."

Marines in *Horace A. Bass*, *Diachenko* (APD 123) and *Wantuck* (APD 125) climbed into the LCVPs that would carry them to shore. *Fort Marion* (LSD 22) prepared to disgorge three utility landing ships carrying tanks and equipment. At 0540, the cruisers and destroyers inaugurated the third day of shelling Wolmi Do and other targets in and around Inchon. Soon after first light, Marine Corsairs launched from

Badoeng Strait and *Sicily* and once again churned up Wolmi Do with bombs, rockets and machine gun fire. Task Force 77 fighters formed combat air patrols to seaward and scoured the roads behind Inchon for enemy reinforcements and supplies.

Fifteen minutes before L hour, set for 0630, two of the ungainly LSMRs began an ear-splitting, 2,000-rocket barrage of the reverse slope of Radio Hill on Wolmi Do. Their object was to destroy any remaining mortar positions and prevent reserves from reaching the defenders of the island. Commander Doss's third ship, *LSMR 403*, moved in front of the

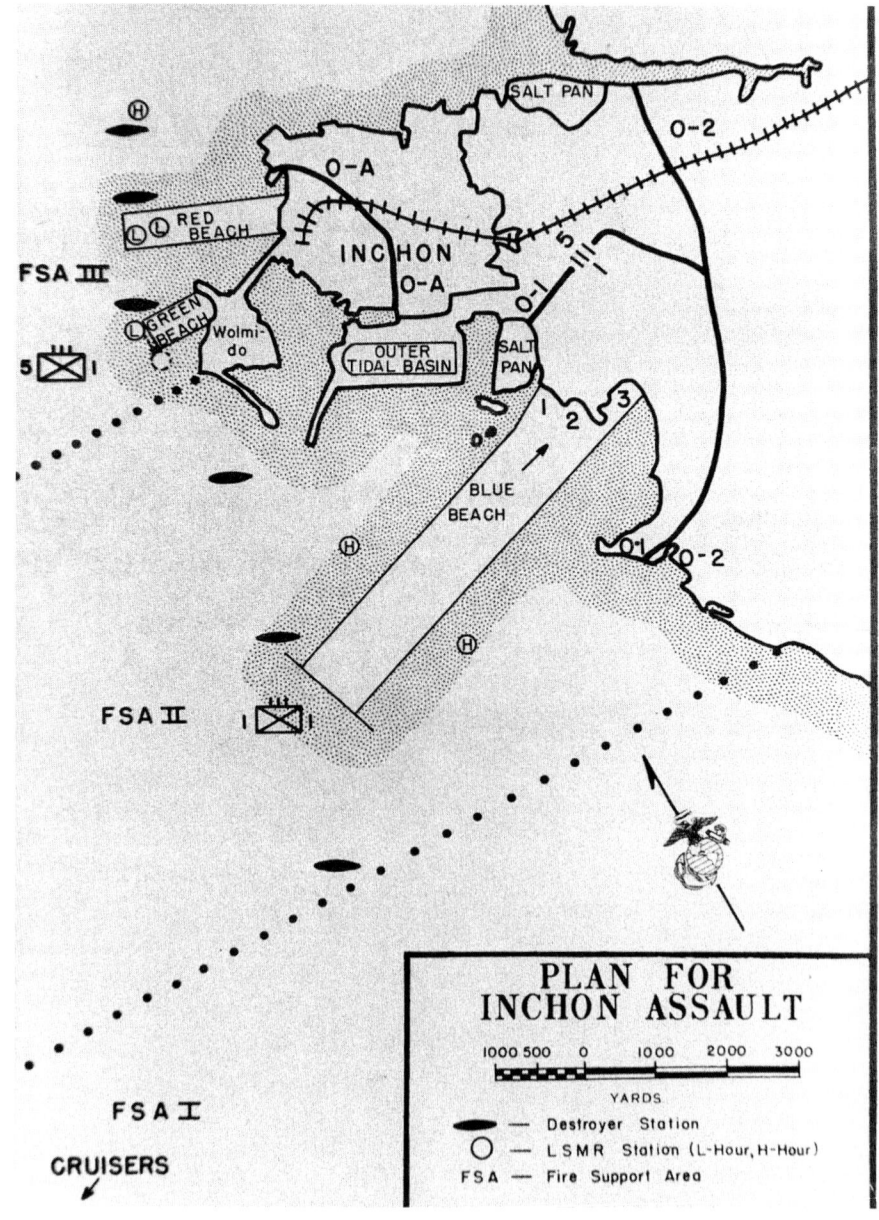

Plan for the Inchon assault showing the three beaches and the planned positions for gunfire support destroyers and LSMRs.

USMC

With the first waves safely ashore on Wolmi Do, General MacArthur and several of his key officers share a light moment on the bridge of *Mount McKinley* (AGC 7). Standing behind MacArthur are (left to right) Rear Admiral Doyle, Brigadier General Edwin K. Wright and Major General Edward Almond, Commander of the X Corps.

111-SC-348448 courtesy NHC

LCVPs on their way to the shore and raked Green Beach with rockets and 40mm fire. That done, signalmen on the control vessel lowered flags signaling the assault. The coxswains in the first wave put their controls at full throttle and the landing craft roared across the line of departure.

To cover the final run into the beach, Corsairs from VMF-214 and VMF-323 screamed over the LCVPs and strafed the shoreline. Two destroyers using proximity-fuzed ammunition scoured the forward slope of Observatory Hill and the waterfront with deadly air bursts of shrapnel.

At 0633, G and H Companies of Colonel Taplett's 3rd Battalion, 5th Marines, stormed ashore. When three men stepped off one LCVP, they sank in water well over their heads. Not wanting a repeat of the tragic experience at Tarawa in World War II when many Marines drowned because they had to move long distances through neck-high water, the boat crews moved their vessels closer to the shore. Succeeding waves brought in the rest of Taplett's Marines and ten M-26 Pershing tanks, including one equipped with a flame-thrower and two more with bulldozer blades.

The Marines advanced rapidly across the island. Company H seized and fortified the Wolmi Do end of the causeway to Inchon, while engineers sprinted onto the roadway to lay an anti-tank minefield. Company G assaulted Radio Hill and by 0655 the stars and stripes flew over that position.

Meanwhile, Taplett landed with his I Company, which moved into areas supposedly secured by the assault units. North Korean troops, hidden in caves on the east side of the island, fired on several I Company squads. When, despite the pleas of a Marine interpreter, the NKPA soldiers refused to surrender, a tankdozer entombed them in their positions.

By 0800, Taplett reported Wolmi Do secured. His leathernecks dug in to fend off any counterattacks and herded the few prisoners of war (POWs) into a dry swimming pool. Some of the NKPA soldiers fought to the last; others, especially local Koreans recently "recruited" by the Communists, readily surrendered. Fanatical enemy troops, however, soon opened up from the nearby islet of Sowolmi Do with light anti-aircraft weapons. A reinforced rifle squad and several tanks rapidly moved against them. Supported by Marine Corsairs, the ground force quickly silenced the enemy guns.

With the outer harbor secured, at the cost of only 17 wounded, the first phase was now over. General MacArthur asked Doyle to send the following message to Task Force 90: "The Navy and Marines have never shone more brightly than this morning." With a large smile, the old soldier then turned to the Army, Navy and Marine officers gathered on Doyle's flagship and said, "That's it. Let's get a cup of coffee." As he drank his cup of thick Navy java, MacArthur penned a message to General Bradley and the other Joint Chiefs: "First phase landing successful with losses slight. All goes well and on schedule."

A Short Interlude

Now began the long, eight-hour wait as the tide receded and rose and the sun began to set in the direction of the Yellow Sea. Not until then could the other Marine units storm Red and Blue beaches. The Navy–Marine task force did not stand idly by during this period. The troops on Wolmi Do improved their fighting positions and naval combatants and aircraft continued to pound the enemy on the mainland.

During this temporary lull in the battle, Admiral Struble's barge came alongside *Mount McKinley* and he asked if anyone would like to tag along with him for a closer look at Wolmi Do and the other beaches. "Certainly," replied MacArthur. Soon, the general, Almond, Shepherd and three other flag-rank officers joined Struble in his barge. After inspecting Green Beach, they moved over toward Red Beach. Shepherd reminded MacArthur that because the boat was less than 1,000 yards from shore, an enemy soldier might "take a pot shot" at the commander of all UN forces in the Korean theater. Struble promptly ordered his coxswain to return to the flagship.

Meanwhile, in response to the seizure of Wolmi Do, the enemy headquarters in Seoul frantically ordered the 70th Regiment near Suwon and the 18th Division, then approaching the Pusan Perimeter, to head toward Inchon. But this action was tardy, because despite two days of bombardment and the garrison commander's warning on the 13th, North Korean authorities did not believe Inchon to be the site of the main amphibious assault. No doubt thanks to the UN deception operations, Communist commanders were fixated on Kunsan until too late. The enemy reinforcements would not be able to reach the battle area by the evening of the 15th, when the Navy–Marine assault forces would hit Red and Blue beaches.

The NKPA garrison at Inchon, composed of the 226th Marine and 918th

A Soviet-made 76.2mm anti-tank gun, emplaced by the enemy on one of the strategic hills overlooking the harbor of Inchon, rests in silence after the battle.

NA 80-G-420387

Coastal Artillery Regiments, was a motley force that included some South Koreans forced into service. The 226th had been further weakened when headquarters earlier sent a large detachment toward Yonghung Do to knock out Clark's guerrillas. In addition, after the loss of Wolmi Do, the best-prepared position in the harbor, the 918th was in bad shape.

The North Korean defensive effort was further hampered by attacks every hour and a half by eight Marine Corsairs, which dropped fragmentation bombs and napalm. The latter ordnance was especially effective against enemy troops, whether dug in or exposed. In addition, to keep pressure on the enemy, twelve Navy carrier aircraft rotated between Yellow Sea combat air patrol and strike operations inland.

One of the latter missions proved to be extremely lucrative. While flying along the road to Suwon, Ensign Eldon W. Brown, Jr., of VF-53 stitched a long row of neatly stacked wooden crates with machine gun fire. When the rounds impacted, there was a massive explosion, the force of which violently jolted Brown's plane. He climbed quickly, but an enveloping cloud of dust and debris passed him at 4,000 feet. In Inchon harbor, miles away, ships rocked at their anchors. *Mount McKinley* radioed the strike leader, Lieutenant Commander Joseph M. Murphy, and asked him, "What the hell happened?" Murphy replied dryly, "We just exploded some ammunition."

On that critical day, 15 September, aircraft carrier *Boxer* arrived on station and ready for battle, culminating two months of Herculean effort by her crew. During that time the ship crossed the vast expanse of the Pacific three times, fighting typhoon Kezia on the last passage, to transport badly needed aircraft to UN forces in the Korean theater. But this effort took its toll on a ship that was scheduled for an overhaul before the outbreak of war. Early on the 15th, a reduction gear in the engineering plant suffered a

Engine room personnel, often called the "black gang" or "snipes," had to use all their skills to maintain speed to make sure that their ships arrived on time off Inchon.

NA 80-G-419918

31

major casualty. With no time to lose, the chief engineer and his engine room crew, or "snipes," used their skills and experience to coax 26 knots out of the damaged propulsion system. Through their efforts, *Boxer* was able to join Task Force 77 and launch her first air strike on time in support of the Inchon landing.

As the day wore on, elements of Naval Beach Group 1's Amphibious Construction Battalion—the Seabees—came in with the tide. Off Wolmi Do, they began building a pontoon dock and causeway, but the vicious tides carried away two sections. Despite this setback, the Seabees completed the pontoon causeway in time for the twilight assault. Meanwhile, other Seabees crossed Wolmi Do. They would advance with Taplett's men an hour after the Red Beach landing to determine the extent of damage to the harbor facilities and sea walls.

At 1445, for the second time that day, Doyle ordered his signalmen to communicate the order to the amphibious force, "Land the landing force." To prepare the beaches for the 1730 H hour, Higgins's destroyers and cruisers increased the tempo of their

fire. *Toledo* and *Rochester* slammed salvos of eight-inch rounds into the roads east of Inchon, creating a gauntlet of steel for enemy reinforcements trying to reach the city. The British cruisers blasted the area around Blue Beach while *De Haven* and *Lyman K. Swenson* shelled the buildings near Red Beach. The structures near the waterfront belched fire and smoke. Navy Skyraiders and Marine Corsairs, whose missions were coordinated by a team from Tactical Air Control Squadron 1 in *Mount McKinley*, added their firepower to the maelstrom.

Meanwhile, off Red Beach, the 1st and 2nd Battalions of the 5th Marine Regiment climbed down rope nets draped on the sides of *Henrico* (APA 45) and *Cavalier* (APA 37) and joined their comrades crowding into the LCVPs and LCMs bobbing alongside. In front of Green Beach, the men of the 11th Marines prepared to go ashore. Farther south, the 1st Marines squeezed into LVTs for the long ride over the mud flats to Blue Beach.

For many of these Marine veterans of World War II amphibious assaults, the Inchon operation was different. In the bottom of each landing craft were two long

planks that the men could use to reach shore if their vessels got stuck in the mud. Other landing craft carried wooden or aluminum ladders with hooks at the top for scaling sea walls. In other boats, Marines stood by with sledgehammers to pound grappling hooks attached to cargo nets into the sea walls.

During the 20 minutes before H hour, the shore bombardment force fired as many rounds as it had in the previous nine hours. *Rochester* and *Toledo* plastered the hills of Inchon, while the destroyers scoured the landing areas with air bursts. Like her two sisters off Blue Beach, *LSMR 403* sent 2,000 five-inch rockets, at the rate of 100 per minute, screaming over the heads of the Marines and sailors heading for Red Beach.

Despite all this firepower, the enemy dropped rounds into the wave of approaching boats. Before the fire of a destroyer off Blue Beach knocked out an NKPA gun, rounds from this weapon destroyed one LVT with a direct hit. *Gurke* and close air support planes quickly silenced a high-velocity gun on Observatory Hill that tried to duel with the Americans. Flying a massive ensign, the small, unarmored *LSMR 401* engaged another enemy weapon with her single five-inch gun. Even though the gun crew had to manually ram shells into the breach because of a mechanical problem, they kept up a high rate of fire that scorched paint off the barrel.

Storming Ashore at Red Beach

In this crescendo of exploding bombs, rockets and shells, *Horace A. Bass*, the control ship for Red Beach, gave the signal for assault. Coxswains in the eight LCVPs of the first wave gunned their engines and conned their boats across the line of departure. Corsairs strafing the beach rained 20mm shell casings on the sailors and Marines in the landing craft.

The assault forces welcomed all of this extra firepower. The causeway on the right flank of Red Beach reminded Marine Captain Francis I. "Ike" Fenton, Jr., Commander of Company B, 1st Battalion, 5th Marines, of the bloody World War II battle of Tarawa. Fenton considered the worst—if the enemy occupied the causeway "we were going to have a tough time making that last 200 yards to the beach."

At 1731, the first LCVP hit the sea wall just ahead of the others in the boat wave. Coxswains skillfully used their engines to hold their boats in place as Marines tossed grenades over the wall. Amidst the explosions, ladders clattered against the rocks and riflemen scrambled "over the top." NKPA machine gunners in the few bunkers still unscathed sprayed the top of this rampart, cutting down some leathernecks and pinning others near the sea wall. The Marines had landed, but just barely.

Nearby, a Navy coxswain rammed his LCVP into a breach in the sea wall. The Marines stormed ashore right under a machine gun, fortunately silent, which protruded from a pillbox. This platoon from Company A quickly grenaded the position and six wounded Koreans stumbled out to surrender. They rapidly cleared nearby trenches, advanced into town and secured the massive Asahi Brewery on the flank of Cemetery Hill. At the base of the Wolmi Do causeway, Company E occupied the Nippon Flour Company compound.

Not everything at Red Beach went so well. Most of Company A was pinned down and the second wave troops crashed in amongst them. First Lieutenant Baldomero Lopez silenced one pillbox and moved to attack a second when an enemy burst hit him. Lopez fell on the grenade he was about to throw, sacrificing his life to save his men. The NKPA gunners continued to fire, killing two more Marines. Company A finally destroyed the pillbox, but above them loomed Cemetery Hill. Then, the platoon at the brewery attacked the back side of the hill and captured several dozen dazed enemy infantrymen. These victories had a cost; eight Marines lay dead on the little flat in front of the graveyard knoll and Navy corpsmen tended another 28 wounded leathernecks.

Although the 5th Marines held Cemetery Hill, the NKPA still threatened Red Beach. Observatory and British Consulate hills remained in enemy hands and until they fell, Communist troops could fire directly into the landing area. It was especially critical that the Marines on Red Beach take the high ground, because the assault waves would be followed by the LSTs loaded with ammunition, vehicles and supplies. Without this resupply, it was unlikely that the Marines could hold their positions overnight.

The consolidation of Red Beach continued, but in ragged fashion. One passenger in the fifth wave, New York *Herald-Tribune* reporter Marguerite Higgins, remarked on the scene. She described a "strange sunset combined with the haze of flaming docks" which created a panorama "that a movie audience would have considered overdone." Poor visibility contributed to a breakdown in coordination. The LCVPs of the fourth and fifth waves became intermingled and many touched land in the wrong areas. These boats carried the two infantry companies that were to seize the most important position in Inchon, Observatory Hill. Hindered by battle smoke and a late afternoon drizzle, it took the two companies several minutes to reorganize ashore. One platoon and a mortar section, however, almost immediately struck out for their objective.

Meanwhile, the eight LSTs destined for Red Beach maneuvered offshore. Each ship had embarked only 500 tons of supplies to lighten their loads and thus prevent grounding in the mud flats. All of the LSTs carried the same proportion of food, water, ammunition, fuel and vehicles, ensuring that the loss of any one ship would not be catastrophic. Doyle's staff calculated that the Marines needed a minimum of 3,000 tons of material to hold during the night. The planners also figured that because of the hostile environment of Inchon harbor and expected enemy opposition, two of the

Baldomero Lopez, A United States Marine

1st Lieutenant Baldomero Lopez represented the best of the Korean War-era Marine Corps. Lopez displayed dedication to the Marine Corps, concern for his men, dynamic combat leadership, personal bravery and a willingness to sacrifice his life for his fellow leathernecks.

The son of an orphaned Spanish immigrant, Lopez enlisted in the U.S. Navy during World War II. He served with distinction until the service discovered that he was underage, which mandated his discharge. Undeterred, Lopez applied for and was admitted to the U.S. Naval Academy. Graduating in Class 1948-A on 6 June 1947, 2nd Lieutenant Lopez entered the Marine Corps. Because he had boxed at the Academy, he earned the nickname "Punchy." He served with the Marines in North China and then joined the 1st Marine Division at Camp Pendleton, California.

Lopez was scheduled for schooling at Quantico, Virginia, when the Commandant of the Marine Corps ordered the Marine Brigade at Pendleton to ship out for Korea. In the words of a fellow Marine officer, Lopez "couldn't stand it. Before the brigade sailed, Punchy swore he would move heaven and earth and get out to us." Sure enough, Lopez was among the replacements from the States when the brigade returned to Pusan after the Naktong battles to refit for Inchon. The eager officer, now a 1st Lieutenant, took command of the 3rd Platoon, Company A, 5th Marines.

Company A made one of the initial assaults at Red Beach. Since Lopez was the only platoon leader without combat experience, the company commander placed the other two rifle platoons in the first wave and his in the second. Despite this precaution, two of the three platoons, including Lopez's, were soon pinned down just over the sea wall. Automatic weapons fire from two pillboxes crisscrossed the area. With other waves coming in, Lopez knew that the situation called for decisive action.

In the face of enemy fire, Lopez led a fire team in

NA 127-GK-234I-A 3190

First Lieutenant Baldomermo Lopez, USMC, scales the sea wall at Red Beach. Minutes after this photo was taken, Lopez sacrificed his life to save his own men and earned the Medal of Honor.

an attack on the two positions. The intrepid officer silenced one bunker with a grenade. Just as he pulled the pin of another grenade, a burst of machine gun fire hit him in the chest and right arm. Badly wounded, he dropped the grenade and its arming handle flew off. The entire fire team was now at risk. Shouting "Grenade!" the lieutenant swept the live ordnance against his side. Lopez smothered the explosion with his own body, sacrificing his life for the lives of his men.

In recognition of this selfless act, the Navy Department awarded 1st Lieutenant Baldomero Lopez the Medal of Honor. His courage and self-sacrifice are remembered by fellow Marines when they serve with USNS *Baldomero Lopez*, a maritime prepositioning ship named in his honor in 1985 by the Secretary of the Navy.

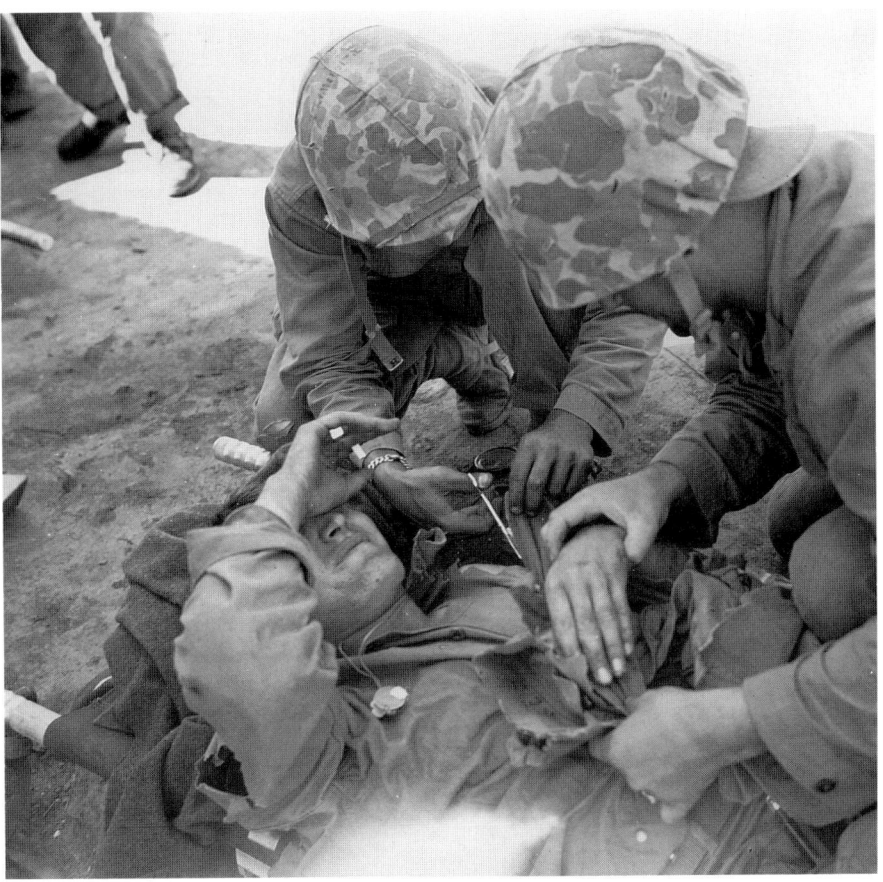

eight ships would be lost.

At 1630, in the wake of the assault waves, *LST 859* crossed the line of departure. She was followed at five-minute intervals by her seven sisters. The LST skippers knew this would be a difficult approach, even in a nonbattle situation, and what they saw ahead of them heightened their anxiety. Gun flashes from the battle at Cemetery Hill domintated the north end of Red Beach. Large groups of Marines hugged the waterfront in the center of the beach, apparently unable to advance inland.

By the time the second ship, *LST 975*, crossed the line, *LST 859* was already taking fire. Communist gunners on Observatory Hill sprayed the landing ships with heavy machine gun rounds, and rifle bullets clanged on their superstructures. NKPA mortars firing from within the city quickly struck several ships. A fire began to blaze among the ammunition trucks on board *LST 914*, but alert sailors and Marines put it out with CO_2 canisters and fog dispensers. A burst of automatic weapon fire holed eight drums of gasoline on *LST 857*, and the deck ran with the volatile fuel. In response, the LSTs wildly swept the beachhead with their three-inch, 40mm and 20mm guns in an attempt to stop the enemy fusillade.

Ashore, the 2nd Battalion's Weapons and Headquarters companies came under intense "friendly" fire from the LSTs. These units, which had not yet suffered casualties, soon counted 1 killed and another 23 wounded. The platoon on Cemetery Hill abandoned the crest and harbor face for the Inchon side, preferring to confront the NKPA heavy machine guns on Observatory Hill rather than the LSTs' weapons. Some Navy LST gunners, however, were on target, destroying a North Korean automatic weapon firing at the men on Cemetery Hill.

Despite some disorganization and both enemy and friendly fire, the 5th Marines continued to move forward. Company E took British Consulate Hill at 1845 as the lone rifle platoon and mortar section seized a portion of Observatory Hill. By 2000, and after a sharp fire fight, Fenton's Company B secured half of the hill. Company D occupied the rest of the position, even though a Communist machine gun killed 1 Marine and wounded 4 others, including the unit's medical corpsman. This sailor refused evacuation until he had treated the wounds of his comrades and ensured their safety.

The Vital LST

The Tank Landing Ship (LST), which proved so crucial to UN success at Inchon, was developed during World War II to deploy tanks, vehicles and critical supplies directly onto assault beaches soon after infantry troops stormed ashore. The ships used a ballast system that allowed them to operate effectively on the open ocean, in shallow coastal waters and on the beach. The LST had a 328-foot length and 50-foot beam and could carry a 2,100-ton load. These ships were the stars of many World War II amphibious operations, and their crews proudly served in them; but because the LSTs could only muster 10 knots of speed, sailors sometimes referred to them as "large, slow targets."

Because of defense cutbacks, by January 1950, only 135 of the 1,051 LSTs America produced during the war remained in commission worldwide. The Shipping Control Administration, Japan (SCAJAP), an occupation agency responsible for inter-island trade and the return of Japanese POWs from other parts of Asia, operated another 39 LSTs. A few others served the U.S. Army in Japanese waters.

Soon after the sudden outbreak of war in Korea, the Navy feverishly concentrated LSTs in Far Eastern waters. These vessels would be essential to the transportation of vehicles and supplies from Japan and to MacArthur's amphibious operations in Korea. Vice Admiral C. Turner Joy, Commander U.S. Naval Forces, Far East, quickly pressed into service the SCAJAP and Army LSTs. Several of these ships were returned to Navy control in the summer of 1950 and were manned largely by reservists recalled to duty. Many of these ships were in a serious state of disrepair.

Lieutenant Erwin E. J. Hauber, Executive Officer of *LST 799*, described his former SCAJAP ship as overrun with "rats bigger than footballs" and stinking with the "penetrating odor of fish heads and urine." The American sailors rearmed their LSTs with guns removed from frigates, which the Navy had provided to the Soviet navy in the World War II lend-lease program and the USSR then returned to U.S. control. Test firing these weapons was an adventure; some of the 20mm antiaircraft guns failed to stop firing or "ran away." One gunnery officer feared that a decrepit three-inch gun would explode, so he tied a 45-foot lanyard to the firing key.

The crews of the 17 American-manned LSTs and 30 Japanese-manned SCAJAP LSTs of Rear Admiral James H. Doyle's Task Force 90 performed small miracles to prepare their ships for Operation Chromite. For instance, when Lieutenant (jg) Leslie H. Joslin, MSC, was ordered to set up an operating room on board *LST 898*, the officer and his men turned to. Joslin's resourceful team scrubbed the small, filthy space assigned to them, brought on board a mountain of supplies, "scrounged" medicines from the Army and installed an operating table that they had removed from mothballed U.S. ships tied up at Kobe since World War II. Thanks to the ingenuity and plain hard work of American and Japanese sailors, when *LST 898* and her sister ships departed for Inchon, they were ready for action.

The SCAJAP *LST QO92* beached at Wolmi Do, 19 September 1950. Visually uninspiring, the Navy and SCAJAP LSTs were essential to the success of the Inchon landing.

NA 80-G-426420

Amtracs carry elements of the 1st Marines toward Blue Beach as *LSMR 401*, positioned near Wolmi Do, fires five-inch rockets at enemy gun emplacements ashore.

Taking the Initiative at Blue Beach

Meanwhile, the assault on Blue Beach had gone better. First, several U.S. destroyers and the LSMRs raked Won-do and Tok Am, small bits of land flanking the approach route taken by the landing craft, and the British cruisers shelled high ground just behind the beach. Then, over 170 LVTs, including 18 gun-equipped armored amtracs (LVT(A)s) of the Army's 56th Amphibian Tractor Battalion, moved toward Blue Beach in 25 waves. The first wave, consisting of all the LVT(A)s, crossed the line of departure at 1645. With the help of four guide boats manned by Navy UDTs, the first three waves made landfall where they were supposed to, although some of the LVT(A)s remained just offshore firing on the beach. Confusion, however, soon set in among the remaining waves. Established procedures called for 32 guide boats to direct a landing of this size, instead of the four available. Rain squalls and smoke from the fighting at Inchon spread across the approach waters off Blue Beach, so succeeding waves could not guide on the first three. Visibility degenerated so quickly that the primary control ship could not even see the landing area. In addition, unanticipated crosscurrents threw many of the amtracs off course.

A number of the more experienced amphibious warfare officers realized that a disaster could occur if they did not take bold action. One such Marine, Major Edwin H. Simmons, a veteran of World War II Pacific landings, grew concerned when the LVT in which he was embarked cut across several boat lanes. Simmons pulled out his map, sought out the LVT driver, and asked him if he had a compass. "Search me," replied the Marine, a recently recalled reservist, "six weeks ago I was driving a truck in San Francisco." Many of the other amtracs were manned by inexperienced crews and because the craft had been hastily pulled out of storage some lacked radios and other essential equipment.

Despite these handicaps, company-grade Navy and Marine officers took the initiative to restore order and put the troops ashore at the best locations. Even though the amtracs landed most of the 1st Battalion, 1st Marines, two miles to the left of their

designated beach, others disgorged their passengers close to intended landing areas near the sea wall. Thirty minutes after H hour, the units at Blue Beach started moving inland.

For a second time that day, the senior UN commanders decided they needed a closer look at Inchon. In the fading daylight and with mortar rounds exploding in the water nearby, Admiral Struble's barge brought Generals MacArthur, Shepherd and Almond alongside the sea wall at Blue Beach. A Marine noncomissioned officer bellowed, with characteristic directness, "Lay off, you stupid bastards! We're going to blast a hole in the wall!" With equal vigor the coxswain retorted, "*This* is Admiral Struble's barge!" The leatherneck responded,

"I don't give a shit whose barge it is, get it clear before I blow the sea wall!" An amused Struble directed the coxswain to back off immediately. Thirty seconds later, a large section of sea wall was blown sky high.

Meanwhile, the Marines at Blue Beach pressed on toward their objectives. On the right flank, an LVT silenced a machine gun nest in a tower 500 yards inland and the 3rd Battalion, 1st Marines, seized several commanding hills and forced an NKPA company to flee their well-prepared positions on Tok Am. On the left flank, the regiment's 2nd Battalion killed 50 NKPA soldiers, captured another 15 and secured the large hill east of Inchon, at a cost of 1 Marine killed and 19 wounded.

A Night in Inchon

Marine reinforcements also headed for Green Beach in the twilight. Inchon's severe currents swept off course some of the underpowered amphibious trucks, or DUKWS, which carried the 105mm guns of the 11th Marines's two howitzer battalions. By 2150, however, all of the "ducks" had waddled ashore and the artillerymen had registered the guns to fire in support of the infantry. After these units came two Marine armored companies, equipped

with Pershing tanks, which rumbled across the causeway and prepared to push toward Kimpo and Seoul.

During the night, *Lyman K. Swenson* and other destroyers and cruisers of the bombardment force fired star shells over the Red Beach perimeter so that the Marines could detect enemy movement. Not all sightings, however, resulted in combat. In the light of one illumination round, Captain Ike Fenton, who was relieving himself at the time, reacted

with surprise when a heavily armed enemy soldier emerged from a hole at his feet. Instead of attacking the startled American officer, the North Korean bowed deeply and surrendered his weapon.

Throughout the night, Navy surgeons and corpsmen of the 1st Marine Division and medical personnel in the LSTs at Red Beach tended the wounded, whose numbers were far below the 300 projected by Doyle's staff. The joint task force suffered 174 wounded in action and 14

Navy Seabees (left to right) Electrician's Mates Troy Edwards, Julian Perez and Joseph D. Edson install floodlights on Red Beach at night on the 15th so that naval forces can sustain their critical over-the-shore logistics operations.

USN 420068

nonbattle injuries. The improvised operating room set up by the surgical team in *LST 898* treated only 42 military and 32 civilian cases. One man was missing and another 21 had been killed in action.

As 15 September ended, it was clear to all that the landing had succeeded. The joint task force had sustained relatively few casualties and lost only two planes (whose pilots were recovered). General Shepherd, a veteran of many landing operations, credited much of this success to the Task Force 90 commander: "Doyle is a great commander and is the best amphibious naval officer I have ever met."

Objective: Seoul

UN forces were now firmly ashore, but the seizure of Inchon was only the opening phase of the campaign to cut off the North Korean Army and liberate South Korea. The next step was to capture Seoul, whose military, political and psychological importance was paramount. Critical to this effort was the fleet's ability to keep pumping reinforcements, transportation resources, ammunition, fuel and supplies into the ever-expanding beachhead.

By the time the LSTs backed off Red Beach with the rising tide on the 16th, the men of Naval Beach Group 1 and the Marine Shore Party Battalion had unloaded 4,000 tons of sup-

(continued on p. 41)

Two days after the initial assault at Inchon, Seabees unload attack cargo ship *Alshain* (AKA 55) landing craft onto the pontoon dock built by the naval constructionmen at Wolmi Do.

USN 420358

Over-the-Beach Logistics

The success or failure of an amphibious operation often depends on how soon the assault forces get resupplied with ammunition, weapons, vehicles, food and fuel. It is equally important for naval logistics forces to keep supplies and troop reinforcements flowing into the beachhead. If they do not, the enemy might push friendly forces into the sea or prevent a breakout from the coast. At Inchon, the lack of adequate port facilities or sea room in which to stage logistics ships made it essential that the naval logistics forces rapidly move supplies "over the beach."

The Navy, the Marine Corps and the Army had developed sophisticated methods and organizations for over-the-beach logistics support based on their experiences in the Pacific in World War II. Naval Beach Group 1, commanded by Captain Watson T. Singer, included beachmasters and small boat units that, along with the 1st Marine Division's Shore Party Battalion led by Lieutenant Colonel Henry P. Crowe, directed the movement of supplies to the beach and then inland. Watson's group also included UDTs that cleared obstacles and Seabees responsible for reconstructing the harbor installations and initially operating the port. The Army's 2nd Special Engineer Brigade, which had supported MacArthur's campaigns in the southwest Pacific during World War II, took over port operations from the naval units.

On the afternoon of the 15th, the Seabees built a large pontoon dock and causeway at Green Beach on Wolmi Do. After the evening landing, some of Singer's sailors and Crowe's Marines had to unload, organize and distribute the supplies from the eight LSTs temporarily immobilized on Red Beach on the evening's high tide. Bringing order out of the dark and chaotic night challenged Crowe, who came up through the ranks and was decorated for heroism at Guadalcanal and Tarawa. Enemy snipers in Inchon shot at Crowe's leathernecks and Singer's sailors, outlined as they were in the glare of the floodlights installed by the Seabees. Nonetheless, the men continued to toil throughout the long night to accomplish their vital mission. All of the LST captains withdrew their emptied ships on the morning's high tide.

By the 19th, one day after the 2nd Special Engineer Brigade took over port operations, the Navy, Marine and Army shore parties had unloaded every ship of the first echelon. Army engineers and the Seabees also had trains operating almost eight miles inland. Once the air strip at Kimpo was opened for business, Air Force transports flew in critical aviation gas and ordnance for the Marine aircraft operating there.

By the 22nd, the multiservice logistics forces had pushed ashore a staggering amount of material: 25,512 tons of cargo, 6,629 vehicles and 53,882 troops. As a result, MacArthur's assault forces were able to seize their lodgement ashore, defend it from counterattack and speedily break out of the coastal enclave.

Four "high-and-dry" LSTs disgorge supplies onto Red Beach on or about 16 September.

plies and equipment. Another nine fully loaded LSTs soon replaced the first group on the beach and the resupply process continued unabated. Other logistics ships and craft disembarked material onto the pontoon dock installed by the Seabees.

Early on the morning of the 16th, a column of six North Korean T-34 tanks rumbled down the road toward Inchon. Two flights of VMF-214 Corsairs operating from *Sicily* pounced on the Soviet-built armored vehicles about a mile short of Marine lines. Even though enemy antiaircraft fire turned one plane into a fireball, the other F4Us destroyed or heavily damaged half of the enemy force. Still, the intrepid Communist tankers kept on coming toward the ridge-line fighting positions of the 5th Marines. Suddenly, Marine Pershing tanks crested the rise, chose their targets and destroyed the rest of the T-34s with accurate fire.

The way now clear of the enemy, the infantrymen of the 1st Marines and the 5th Marines advanced and around 0730 linked up east of Inchon. South of town, the leathernecks occupied an abandoned coastal artillery position and captured a 120mm mortar battery. At the same time, General Smith ordered the 3rd Battalion, 1st KMC Regiment, into Inchon to mop up enemy troops and sympathizers, whose hiding places local civilians gladly revealed. Incensed by civilian reports

American troops inspect a Soviet-made T-34 tank destroyed by Marine fire on the road from Inchon to Seoul. Allied ground, air and naval gunfire defeated every enemy armor attack against the Inchon beachhead.   NA 80-G-421166

South Korean marines attach a prisoner-of-war identification tag to a North Korean soldier who tried to evade capture in Inchon by donning civilian clothes. The ROK marines, responsible for "mopping up" the city, also tracked down and severely dealt with Communists involved in atrocities.   NA 80-G-426429

of Communist atrocities, for the remainder of the day the South Korean Marines ruthlessly sought out the North Koreans and other "subversives."

As UN forces secured Inchon and strengthened the beachhead on the 16th, the UN command took other steps to engage the North Korean army. General Walker's Eighth Army attacked out of the Pusan Perimeter, working to prevent the early withdrawal of NKPA units from the southern front. Then, the U.S. Army and ROKN mounted an operation to cut the north–south road at Changsa-Dong on the peninsula's east coast. A Korean LST attempted to land a guerrilla force, but the ship grounded and broached just offshore. The irregulars finally made it to the beach, only to be attacked by a nearby North Korean garrison. The operation a failure, the battleship *Missouri* and cruiser *Helena* and Air Force F-51 Mustangs hit the enemy with their fire so another LST could extract the guerrillas.

On the 17th, the North Koreans counterattacked the UN beachhead at Inchon, so Communist reinforcements might have time to reach Seoul. Early that morning, the North Korean air force made its one and only assault on the amphibious force off Inchon. A pair of YAK fighters dove on the warships anchored south of Wolmi Do. Except for a lone sailor on sentry duty at the stern

of the cruiser *Rochester*, who fired his rifle at the planes, the crew of the cruiser was caught off guard. The enemy planes dropped several bombs on the Americans but the only weapon that hit a ship failed to explode. The YAKs then strafed HMS *Jamaica*, mortally wounding one seaman and hitting two others. The Royal Navy took its revenge, splashing one of the attackers with fire from four-inch guns and automatic weapons. The cruiser's skipper, Captain Jocelyn C.

S. Salter, RN, later felt that it was "foolhardy" of the North Koreans "to go for two cruisers when they had a choice of transports and freighters galore."

As that futile attack ended, an NKPA rifle battalion supported by a platoon of T-34s advanced against the lines of the 5th Marines. The North Korean units, which made no reconnaissance of UN positions, moved into a trap. The 5th Marines quickly destroyed the tank column. To the south, Colonel

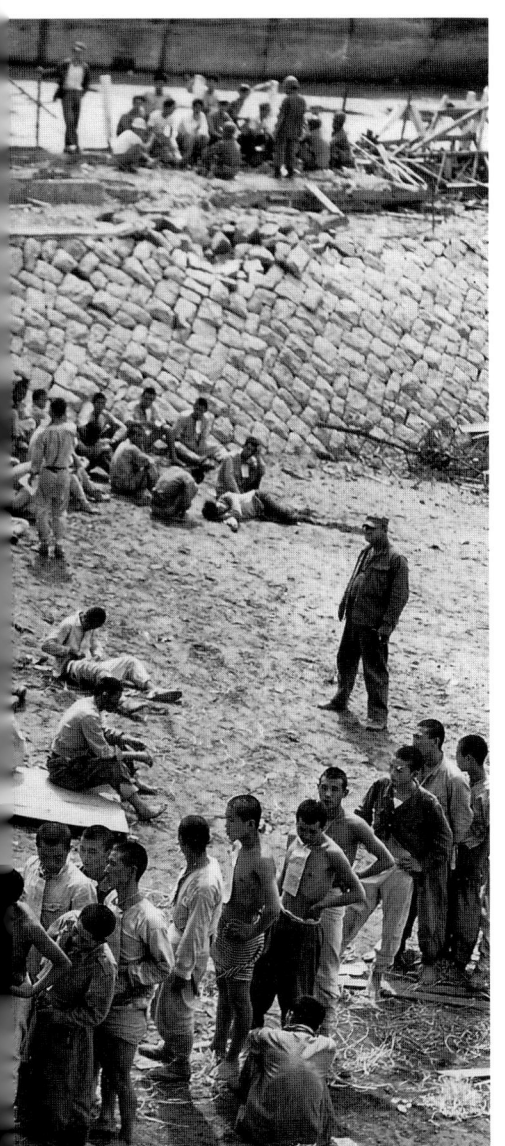

Lewis B. Puller's leathernecks had a tougher fight. Elements of the 1st Marine Regiment, with the help of five Corsairs, fought their way through a heavily fortified defile on the road to Seoul.

Much to the distress of General Smith, MacArthur went ashore that morning and insisted on traveling just behind the front line, at one point directing his jeep driver to a ridge crest to observe a fire fight. Smith was greatly relieved when CIN-CUNC returned safely to *Mount McKinley*, particularly when he learned that his Marines had flushed seven heavily armed NKPA soldiers from the culvert on which MacArthur's jeep idled as he viewed some burning T-34s.

With the NKPA attack spent, the 5th Marines seized the south end of Kimpo air base and a KMC battalion advanced to cover their left flank. North Korean counterattacks that night failed to dislodge the Americans from Kimpo. Artillery

American Marines inspect a North Korean Ilyushin IL-10 "Shturmovik" (Soviet-built) attack bomber seized when U.S. forces overran Kimpo airfield. Except for one foray against the fleet, the North Korean air force could do little to help the defenders of Inchon. The Allies had clear superiority in the air.

NA 80-G-420388

fire from the 11th Marines and small arms fire decimated the ranks of the enemy infantry forces moving against the air base perimeter.

On the 18th, the 3rd Battalion, 1st Marines, stormed Hill 123. Assistance in this attack came from HMS *Kenya*, which poured 300 six-inch rounds on the enemy. Still unbeaten, NKPA gunners inflicted 30 casualties on the Americans when they shelled the slopes of the hill. Throughout the hour-long barrage, the senior naval medical officer present, Lieutenant Robert J. Fleischaker, MC, moved about the hill to treat the wounded, without regard for his safety. The Navy awarded Fleischaker the Bronze Star for his bravery under fire.

In support of the 5th Marines, the cruisers *Rochester* and *Toledo* and U.S. Navy

American and South Korean troops process North Korean prisoners of war on Wolmi Do.

NA 80-G-420390

Skyraiders bombarded Communist forces on both sides of the Han River northwest of Kimpo. Despite these heavy attacks, the naval aviators reported that the enemy units were "still active."

That same day, the Joint Task Force 7 transports began disembarking several Army units. The 7th Infantry Division's 32nd Infantry Regiment landed and advanced to cover the 1st Marine Division's right flank. The 96th Field Artillery Battalion and the 2nd Engineer Special Brigade also came ashore, with the engineers relieving the KMC battalion in Seoul.

On 19 September, the 1st Marine Division continued to advance on Seoul. The 5th Marines, still within supporting distance of the task force cruisers, prepared to cross the Han north of the capital. To the south, the 1st Marines began a three-day battle for the industrial suburb of Yongdungpo.

Critical close air support for this fight would come from VMF-212 and night-fighting squadron VMF(N)-542, which flew into Kimpo from Japan that day. Marine Brigadier General Thomas J. Cushman, the X Corps tactical air commander, directed these units. FEAF's Combat Cargo Command, with C-54 and Fairchild C-119 Flying Boxcars, also began flying ammunition and aviation gas into Kimpo on the 19th. The experienced Air Force cargo handlers of the 1st Combat Support Unit

(Provisional) quickly unloaded and pushed forward the vital material.

The UN advance toward Seoul continued on the 20th and the 21st. After an initial setback, Marine LVTs carrying the 3rd Battalion, 5th Marines, crossed the Han River and, with the assistance of *Sicily*'s VMF-214 fighters, established a lodgement on the far bank. The ground force received a welcome re-

inforcement when the Army's 31st Infantry Regiment, the ROK 17th Infantry Regiment and the 7th Marines came ashore at Inchon. The 6th Fleet's attack transport *Bexar* (APA 237) and attack cargo ship *Montagu* (AKA

(Left to right) Airman William J. Ewsuk, Aviation Ordnanceman 2nd Class Francis L. Diamond and Airman Joseph F. Bellina arm a Vought F4U Corsair of Fighter Squadron 24 on board *Boxer* (CV 21). Success in combat depended on the professional skill and plain hard work of everyone on the Navy team.   NA 80-G-420997

"Corsair," by Herbert Hahn, depicts Fighter Squadron 63 F4Us hitting enemy positions with rocket fire to clear the way for American tanks advancing on Seoul.

Navy Art Collection KN 18959

Heavily armed Corsairs of Fighter Squadron 24 and Douglas AD Skyraiders of Attack Squadron 65 warm up prior to the launching of another ground support mission.

Bob Lawson

98) had completed the long journey from the Mediterranean to deliver one of the 7th Marines' battalions.

As these reinforcements moved up to the front, the Communists struck back. On the 21st, NKPA troops crossed the Han and assaulted South Korean marine positions northwest of Kimpo airfield. Carrier aircraft and the naval gunfire of *Toledo* obliterated the Communist attacking force. In addition, Navy Skyraiders reduced enemy resistance in Suwon before the 7th Division's Reconnaissance Company occupied the city.

As these actions took place, as planned, Admiral Struble dissolved Joint Task Force 7 and turned over operational control of Chromite to General Almond. Almond desperately wanted to take Seoul by the 25th—exactly three months after the North Korean invasion. He believed that the Communists must be on the brink of collapse. General Smith was not as optimistic.

The leathernecks assaulted Seoul's western defenses on the 22nd and found enemy resistance especially strong. The Seoul garrison now included several heavily armed and well-led NKPA units that had been rushed to the city from all directions. The Marines had to battle their way through Seoul, house to house, street to street. The fighting battered the South Korean capital. Marine casualties, light up to that point, steadily mounted. Navy surgeons and corpsmen, especially the latter who often exposed themselves to enemy fire when helping wounded Marines, paid a heavy price for their bravery. By midday on the 24th, every corpsman with F Company, 5th Marines, had either been killed or seriously wounded. NKPA soldiers cut down Hospital

U.S. Marines focus their attention on North Korean snipers during the costly house-to-house fight for Seoul, the South Korean capital.

NA W&C #1422

Corpsman 3rd Class James J. Ergesitz as he pulled a wounded Marine from a fire-swept slope. Communist mortar rounds hit the 1st Battalion, 5th Marines' aid station and wounded a surgeon, Navy Lieutenant Francis T. H'Doubler, MC. He continued to treat casualties until incapacitated by another wound. Chief Hospital Corpsman Wayne D. Austin, already hit in the face and ankle, took over and tended 40 more men before being relieved. Only when a replacement arrived did Chief Austin, wounded once more, consent to evacuation. For his actions, Austin received the Navy Cross.

General Almond, dissatisfied with the Marine progress through the city, moved the 32nd Infantry

and the 17th ROK Infantry across the Han to flanking positions. The enemy continued to fight with determination and skill, but Almond was persuaded that their resistance would be short lived. Just before midnight on the 25th, he declared Seoul liberated.

To the leathernecks and soldiers in the city this was a cruel joke, because the NKPA still held 60 percent of the city and that night launched three counterattacks. Despite taking heavy casualties, the North Koreans stubbornly hung on until 28 September. Even the next day, when General MacArthur and President Rhee presided over a ceremony returning the capital of the Republic of Korea to its people, attendees could hear the sound of

46

Marines prepare to raise the U.S. flag over Seoul on 26 September, even though fighting would continue in outlying districts for several more days.

artillery and small arms fire coming from the northern suburbs.

Meanwhile, General Walker's 8th Army had broken out of the Pusan Perimeter, raced to the northwest and joined forces with Almond's X Corps. When the 1st Cavalry Division's legendary 7th Cavalry Regiment met elements of the 7th Infantry Division near Osan, on the morning of 27 September, the campaign for South Korea was almost over. Of the 70,000 North Korean soldiers engaged at Pusan, much less than half escaped death or capture. Only 30,000 men, with virtually no heavy weapons, recrossed the 38th parallel into North Korea. A better coordinated attack by the Eighth Army that concentrated on isolating forces, rather than racing to Inchon, might have netted the entire NKPA. Nonetheless, the bloody campaign in South Korea and the hasty retreat from Pusan had exhausted and demoralized the survivors of the once mighty NKPA invasion force. Of paramount importance, the UN forces that stormed ashore at Inchon had achieved their primary purpose—the liberation of the Republic of Korea.

7th Infantry Division and 1st Cavalry Division soldiers shake hands and hold up unit insignia to mark the 28 September linkup of the Inchon and Pusan forces south of Suwon.

Conclusion

The amphibious assault at Inchon showed how the skillful use of naval force enables theater commanders to bring decisive power to bear on enemy nations touched by the sea. The cruisers, destroyers, frigates and carriers, along with UN air forces, first secured control of the Yellow Sea, the Sea of Japan and the air spaces over these waters. This unexpected display of strength led North Korea's international Communist supporters to reconsider their policies regarding the Korean peninsula.

After eliminating the North Korean air force, UN ship- and land-based air power battered military facilities in North Korea and logistical lines to the Communist troops in South Korea. At the same time, U.S. and Royal Navy warships bombarded NKPA front-line troops and supply routes near the coasts, providing vital support to the U.S. and ROK ground units. Because of post-World War II defense cutbacks, however, the lack of ships, aircraft and material ready for combat almost doomed the UN cause in Korea in July and August 1950.

Control of the sea and the ability to assemble and organize enough merchantmen, transports and cargo ships allowed the UN command to move reinforcements to the Far East from all parts of the world. General MacArthur, the theater commander and an experienced practitioner of amphibious warfare, knew that he now possessed a clear advantage over his enemy. He was able to choose the best time and place to strike the rear of the North Korean army. If success crowned his efforts, he would liberate South Korea.

The naval forces in the Far East, under the command of Admirals Joy, Struble and Doyle, then worked to execute MacArthur's concept. Despite the difficulties in gathering relevant intelligence and assembling the variety of units needed, these veteran commanders and their expert staffs quickly planned the assault of a site that presented many physical problems. They then coordinated the necessary naval, air and ground force for the complex operation.

Almost every type of naval unit contributed to the victory at Inchon. Carrier-based Navy and Marine planes and surface combatants prepared the battlefield and, in conjunction with the Air Force, helped to deceive the enemy about the actual invasion area. Continued attacks by naval air and surface forces throughout the landing, consolidation and breakout phases of Chromite added considerably to the woes of the North Korean defenders. Other naval units cleared Inchon's approach waters of mines. Most importantly, the sailors manning the assault ships and craft and the Marines storming the enemy's positions exhib-

NA 80-G-423716

Rear Admiral James H. Doyle, who one Marine general regarded as "the best amphibious naval officer I have ever met," awards Silver Star medals for bravery to landing craft sailors (left to right) Seaman Chancey H. Vogt, Seaman William H. Tagan, Engineman Fireman Richard P. Vinson and Seaman Apprentice Paul J. Gregory.

ited the skill and bravery necessary to the success of any opposed landing. Once ashore, the 1st Marine Division soundly defeated their foes and secured the objectives with typical courage and professional skill.

The Navy, particularly its often forgotten support services, remained critical to the success of the operation. Corpsmen, surgeons and chaplains were on hand to treat the wounded and comfort the dying. The ungainly LSTs provided essential materials and services for the beachhead. The Naval Beach Group's Seabees, UDTs, beachmasters and boat units and the Marine Shore Party kept vehicles, equipment and supplies flowing across the beach. Transports and cargo ships brought in additional U.S. and ROK soldiers and Marines. Oilers, tenders and stores ships supplied combatants on station, enabling the fleet to remain off Inchon and to provide the ground forces with continued naval air and gunfire support.

Often in war, good intelligence, careful planning and bold execution favor one side with relatively light casualties, and this was the case at Inchon. During the first seven days of Chromite, the joint task force counted approximately 70 killed, 470 wounded and five missing. Because of the bloody fighting for Seoul, the toll rose to 600 killed, 2,750 wounded and 65 missing. At the same time, UN forces killed 14,000 North Korean soldiers and captured another 7,000.

Of greater importance, Admiral Struble's joint task force carried out the theater commander's directive to strike the NKPA a lethal blow and drive the aggressors from the Republic of Korea. To General MacArthur, "the Navy and Marines . . . never shone more brightly" than at Inchon.

Acknowledgements

The author would like to acknowledge the efforts of several groups, organizations and individuals who assisted in the preparation of this volume. The staffs of the Prints and Photographs Division and the Map and Geography Division, both of the Library of Congress, the National Archives Still Picture Branch and the Archives Division of the National Air and Space Museum provided critical materials for the project. I am grateful to Dr. Dean C. Allard, Director of Naval History; Captain William D. Vance, USN, Deputy Director; and Dr. William S. Dudley, Senior Historian, for their continued support. The series editor, Dr. Edward J. Marolda, provided useful direction, comment and assistance in preparing this volume. My thanks also go to Brigadier General Edwin H. Simmons, USMC (Ret.), Director of Marine Corps History and Museums; Professor Roger Dingman of the University of Southern California; Dan J. Crawford, Robert V. Aquilina and Amy Cantin, Marine Corps Historical Center; Dr. Vincent A. Transano, Command Historian, Naval Facilities Engineering Command; Anne C. DeAtley, Det 9, 1st Combat Camera Squadron, USAF; and Robert L. Lawson. My coworkers in the Naval Historical Center also provided tremendous assistance in their various specialties, including editor Sandra K. Russell, art director Charles C. Cooney and typesetter and photographer JO1(SW) Eric S. Sesit, Naval Aviation News Branch; Chuck Haberlein and Ed Finney, Photographic Section; Bernard F. Cavalcante, Gina Akers, John L. Hodges, Kathleen M. Lloyd and Mike Walker, Operational Archives Branch; John C. Reilly, Jr., Ship's History Branch; Ella Nargele, Information Security Specialist; Glenn E. Helm and Jean L. Hort, Navy Department Library; S. Gale Munro and the late John Barnett, Navy Art Collection Branch; and Steven D. Hill and Judith A. Walters, Naval Aviation History Branch. The support, advice, information, comments and technical skill provided by my colleagues in the Contemporary History Branch—Jeffery G. Barlow, Robert J. Cressman, Richard A. Russell, Robert J. Schneller and Gary E. Weir—contributed significantly to the success of this project. I also thank my wife, Ruth, who reviewed several drafts and clarified my sometimes awkward and confusing presentation.

About the Author

Curtis A. Utz is a historian in the Naval Historical Center's Contemporary History Branch. He graduated from the University of Maryland where he earned a Bachelor of Arts degree in history in 1984. He served as a historical interpretation technician with the National Park Service and an intern at the Smithsonian's National Air and Space Museum. In 1989, he completed a Master of Arts degree in history at the University of Maryland. Mr. Utz has worked as a free-lance military historian and researcher. He served as a historian with the Contemporary History Branch from 1992 through 1994. Mr. Utz authored the first volume in this series, *Cordon of Steel: The U.S. Navy and the Cuban Missile Crisis*.

Suggested Reading List and Sources

Blair, Clay. *The Forgotten War: America in Korea 1950–1953*. New York: Times Books, 1987.

Cagle, Cdr. Malcom W. and Cdr. Frank A. Manson. *The Sea War In Korea*. Annapolis: Naval Institute Press, 1957.

Field, James A., Jr. *History of United States Naval Operations: Korea*. Washington: GPO, 1962.

Heinl, Robert D. *Victory at High Tide: The Inchon–Seoul Campaign*. Philadelphia: J. B. Lippincott Company, 1967.

Karig, Capt. Walter, Cdr. Malcom W. Cagle and LCdr. Frank A. Manson. *Battle Report, Volume VI: The War in Korea*. New York: Rinehart and Company, Inc., 1952.

Montross, Lynn and Capt. Nicholas A. Canzona. *U.S. Marine Corps Operations in Korea, 1950–1953, Volume II: The Inchon–Seoul Operation*. Washington: GPO, 1955.

In addition to secondary sources, the author used primary materials held in the Naval Historical Center's Operational Archives and Ships' History branches, as well as the Marine Corps Historical Center's Reference Section and Personal Papers Unit.